MOTIVATING
AND PREPARING
BLACK YOUTH
FOR SUCCESS

by Jawanza Kunjufu

AFRICAN AMERICAN IMAGES
Chicago, Illinois

Cover photo by William Hall

Cover design by Eugene Winslow

First Edition
Tenth Printing

DEDICATION

To the youth studying in the library, working on a science project, singing in the church choir, watching television, listening to the radio, and playing basketball; no generation can choose the age or circumstances in which it is born, but through faith and work you must develop your talents and "use yourself up." Because, it is unfortunately true that to be Black in White America requires more than a score of 100 percent, it means scoring 110 percent.

SPECIAL THANKS

Special thanks is given to my wife Rita, for her understanding and editorial assistance. A special thanks is given to Larry Hawkins for the introduction and Eugene Winslow for his editing. Deep respect and appreciation are given to Sanyika Anwisye for the scholarship lended to the book.

TABLE OF CONTENTS

Preface iii

Foreward i

Chapter 1
The Politics of Work 1

Chapter 2
Values as the Foundation for Motivation 15

Chapter 3
Motivation for Success 25

Chapter 4
The Development of Talents into a Career ... 35

Chapter 5
Jobs: The Present and Beyond 45

Chapter 6
How to Become Economically Self-Sufficient 59

Epilogue 67

Footnotes 69

Index 73

FOREWORD

The many problems that plague our youth have no single cure. Jawanza advocates the need to instill motivation, many experts feel the lack of, has created our high dropout rate. There is a growing need to revitalize the educational system across the board. At the same time, there is a sharper need for parents and the Black community to undergo dramatic restructuring of the resources available and attitudes controlling its schools.

The author's point of the anti-intellectual environment of the Black community is indeed a prime target in this proposed restructuring. The ideas and societal perceptions that our students are unable to perform academically must be refuted. As we demand more from students they will achieve academically; our students are as capable as any other students. They must be convinced of that.

Paralleled to the concept of anti-intellectualism is the view that schools are solely responsible for educating students. This leads to the fallacy that only schools can and do teach, and further, to the dangerous assumption that parents need only send their children to school.

Education is the specific responsibility of the *parents*. They are the source, and all other agencies, school, churches and community, are secondary resources that parents and students should make use of. Parents must view this as their responsibility until their child is of age to assume the task of learning.

What exactly should parents be doing for their children? Through a series of deliberately planned activities, parents should give students a sense of self-worth, providing the basis for a value system that equips the child to function in American society. Within this value system the parent helps to shape the concept of service. The concept of community service should not be allowed to disappear when the youth moves away to gain higher education or to work for others. During the "moving away" process, a young person should apply their knowledge and become a producer who in turn provides opportunities for others. This positive, mature outlook by the young person is dependent upon him being encouraged by his parents *early on* to develop that fundamental value of self-worth.

Beyond instilling these strong values, parents must play a key role in monitoring the student's school, the student himself, and the student's environment in order to assure values taught at home have the proper context in which to mature. Parents should insist that schools teach and that students study and learn. Mastery of the tools of learning is crucial. Therefore, the parent must insist that the student is disciplined as a learner. Without discipline and respect, little will be achieved.

Community agencies can be a potent force in the student's educational process. Social agencies, clubs, and sports groups should be viewed as vital to the student and, consequently, to the student's education. Again, the road leads home. It is the parents that must understand and coordinate these talent centers to ensure they support and complement the child's education.

Summers should also be planned to complement the child's learning process. Summers should be considered a prime time for learning, not for working. The work of youth is to learn. Learning about work is, of course, part of the process, but should not be all of it. The confidence necessary to secure a job comes from secure knowledge and a positive self-image. This is acquired over time through education. If students are to be creative and to create, they must spend time learning about the people who build organizations. Students must study the experiences of others to develop their own sense of the importance of learning and the necessity of hard work to achieve. In this way, when they do approach the working world, it will be with the values, attitudes, and premises of achievement.

This point of view will of necessity come from a community perspective. We must find local neighborhood constituencies that, along with parents, motivate Black youth to work. The goal for all of us involved with youth should be to prepare an individual capable of competing internationally, who is socially concerned, and community-based in outlook. We seem to have a diminishing number of agencies and people in our communities to instill collective values, motivation, and talent development. The task for all of us is to remember where we came from, remain informed of where we are, and to reach back and help someone.

Larry Hawkins
Director of Special Programs
and The Institute for Athletics And Education
University of Chicago

PREFACE

I had more difficulty in writing *Motivating and Preparing Black Youth For Success*, than either *Countering The Conspiracy to Destroy Black Boys*, or *Developing Positive Self-Images and Discipline in Black Children*. Part of the problem was deciding for whom the book was to be written. My ultimate desire was to reach the reader between thirteen and twenty-one years of age. I saw vast numbers of young people filled with talents, but with very little motivation or adult guidance. I read studies that postulate large percentages of Black youth may never work. The predicament is that few thirteen to twenty-one year olds may read this book because most read only required school materials.

I also contemplated writing for the primary grade student with hopes of stemming the decline in motivation with each passing year. My reservations lie in the realization that this would place on this age group the difficult task of developing their own motivational techniques. I have resolved the dilemma by appealing to teachers, parents, counselors, administrators, librarians, Upward Bound and Manpower staff, and all concerned adults who interact with youth, to pass this book along to them. I further request that they share my ideas with the primary grade group, so that we can begin being proactive with preventive measures, rather than reactive with crisis intervention and band-aid programs.

I am an advocate of moving from theory to practice. I believe that the majority of people have a good assessment of what the problems are, but few have furnished solutions. All of my books are action oriented; their titles use key words such as *countering, developing*, and this book chooses *motivating* and *preparing*. When I tell people the title of this book, their first response is, "How do we motivate Black youth?" I gather they want me to reduce all my research and pages of the book down to the ABC's of motivating and preparing Black youth for success. I strongly encourage reading all six chapters, which include: (1) "The Politics of Work," (2) "Values as the Foundation for Motivation," (3) "Motivation for Success," (4) "The Development of Talents Into a Career," (5) "Jobs: The Present and Beyond," and (6) "How to Become Economically Self-Sufficient." Those who either don't have the time or the interest in absorbing the details of the book can motivate and prepare Black youth for success by: (a) changing their values from consumption to self-improvement, (b) maintaining their enthusiasm to learn with continued encouragement or questions, (c) making a dedicated effort to identify and develop their talents, and (d) teaching our youth to consider becoming future employers.

There are numerous books on the market concerning the work ethic, employment, and business ventures. Fewer titles are available on values, motivation, and talents. I have found no books that, from a Black youth perspective, combine the above mentioned areas with the sense of direction needed for them to reach their fullest potential.

I realize that my objective for writing this book is much more ambitious than can be achieved by a book alone. I would like for the book to rejuvenate Black youth and reduce the preposterously high Black unemployment rate. But books don't do that; people with vision and ideas do. However, with your help, we can make a positive difference in the Black youth of today and the future of all African-Americans.

Jawanza Kunjufu

Chapter 1
The Politics of Work

It's 8:30 Monday morning. Willie is lying in the bed watching television and dozing off between commercials. He is twenty years old, six feet tall and weighs 170 pounds. His day has been divided between the television and the street corner since age sixteen. Willie was a good student in the primary grades where his natural ability was sufficient, but in the upper grades where discipline and study habits are expected, Willie adhered more to the culture and rigors of the street and its highly influential peer group. Willie does not know in retrospect, whether he dropped out or was pushed out at the first "legal" age of sixteen. Willie knows that both he and school had been together since day care at the ripe age of three, and that thirteen years of being still and listening to ideas unrelated to his world were enough.

His mother has been working at the phone company all of his life; his older brother works at the post office, and his younger sister presently is in college. Willie has never known his father. From time to time, Willie drops into a community center that offers GED training. He has taken several courses but not the test.

There are large numbers of teenagers and young adults who parallel Willie — male, female, younger and older, from two parent affluent homes as well as single parent welfare dwellings.

What actually happened to Willie? When did it happen? What prevented Willie from maintaining his development like his brother and sister? What will happen to Willie's talents while he watches television? Did someone fail Willie? If so, who? Was it the family, school, economy, church, or government? In succeeding chapters we will ask: What does Willie value? How can Willie be motivated? What are Willie's talents? What is the present employment picture for him? How can he become economically self-sufficient?

Let's return to the first question, What happened to Willie and when? I believe the first step toward self-actualization is the development of self-esteem. This becomes extremely significant for Black people because we live in a world controlled by an insecure minority. Eighty percent of the world's population is Black, brown, red or yellow; the remaining twenty percent is White. The White minority have developed the theory of racism, by claiming that their differences make them better. Secure people are comfortable with differences and have no need to demonstrate or prove their superiority. Unfortunately, many Blacks assume the inferior role of the victim and defensively respond to the myths and stereotypes. Our problem commences when we believe the myths and stereotypes are true. Please remember, it was Africans who built the **pyramids and the Grand Lodge of Wa'at, now in the city renamed Luxor.**

As a result, Willie, his peers, parents, and the larger society often believe that Black people are lazy, prefer welfare, and lack qualifications. I advocate that many things are political, i.e.,determined by *interest*. For example, many White historians say that Columbus discovered America, while many Black historians state that Columbus was lost and native Americans, in fact, discovered him. The criteria used to determine which view will be included in the curriculum will probably not be decided on empirical research, but by political interests. If Black children have not read Walter Rodney's, *How Europe Underdeveloped Africa* or Manning Marable's, *How Capitalism Underdeveloped Black America* they may not know that the people who are being classified as lazy provided the labor to make Europe and America rich. Marable states,

> Where would the original accumulation of capital used in Western industry have come from if not from the extraction of wealth from colonies, piracy, and the slave trade. The constant expropriation of surplus created by Black labor is the heart and soul of underdevelopment. Underdevelopment is not the absence of development; it is the inevitable product of an oppressed population's integration into the world market economy and political system. Once "freed," Black Americans were not compensated for their 246 years of free labor to this country's slave oligarchy. The current economic amnesia of the West is therefore no accident, because it reveals the true roots of massive exploitation and human degradation upon which the current world order rests.[1]

Why bring a lazy people to America? Why spend six to nine months on a slave ship incurring expenses for transporting a worthless people? Why not use indentured servants or native

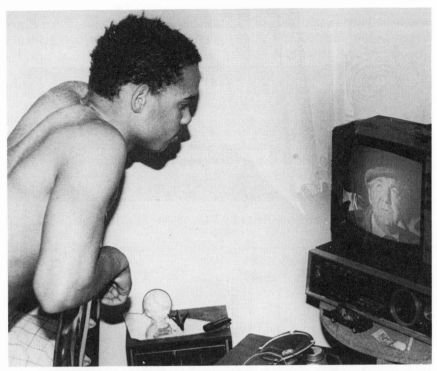

Beyond the streets, radio and television, where can Willie channel his energy and intellect?

Americans? Do you think European slave traders would take slaves without observing their work ethic before the journey? Why accuse a people of being dirty and lacking family cohesiveness and then, during and after slavery, employ Blacks as maids and nannies? Why allow your house and children to be cared for by people lacking competence? Why declare that Blacks don't want to work, when television news shows massive crowds of people, including Blacks, gathered to apply for a few positions that may not even be available. Why should Blacks, who were here "unofficially" in 1619, be compared to illegal aliens who came right off the boat yesterday? America often ignores the fact that its treatment of Blacks has been that of second-class citizens for over 300 years. Why spread the stereotype that welfare is predominantly Black when governmental reports note that of the 35 million who receive financial assistance,

23 million are White and only 12 million are "minorities."[2] The chart listed below illustrates that a "good education" may not insure a "good job" for all people.

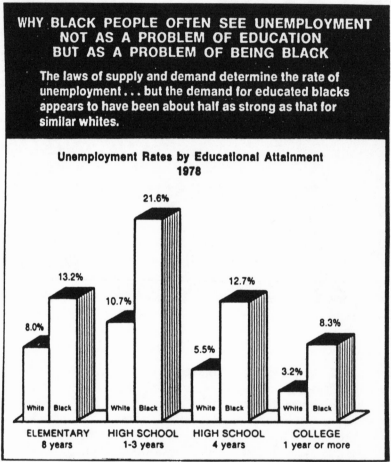

From *Black Power Imperative* by Theodore Cross. Copyright 1984 by Faulkner. Reprinted by permission of the publisher.

Willie's lack of motivation and preparation to work begins with overt and institutional racism, but becomes compounded with low self-esteem, and indifferent adults who perpetuate the self-fulfilling prophecy. These are the "offensive" responses needed to counter the practice of blaming the victim. They become essential because although Willie is not like others such as, the "talented tenth," Willie's brother and sister are progressing. The widening gap between the "haves" and the "have nots" has reached epidemic proportions. Simultaneously, in the Black community are "buppies" (Black urban professionals) and Blacks who have not worked and may never work. One segment of the talented tenth has no desire to help the Black masses and will quickly articulate how the "bootstrap theory" worked for them, and will place failure squarely at the feet of the individual. Large numbers of the talented tenth are not even seen by the masses. They do not live, shop, recreate, fellowship, or educate their children near the masses. Another segment of the talented tenth has good intentions and/or an African worldview, but is having difficulty reaching the masses and providing positive role models.

Youth unemployment over the past two decades has been between 16 and 25 percent. Black youth statistics indicate a rate twice the national average.[3] Major reasons often cited are racial discrimination, teenage pregnancy, distance, and lack of work readiness skills. In the year 2,000, if you're a young man and black, brown or tan, the odds are about two to one that you won't have a job. The largest obstacle facing females of color is teenage pregnancy and inadequate child care. Labor participation rates of young Black women are expected to increase from 55 percent in 1983 to 70 percent by the year 2000.[4] The semi-skilled jobs that appeal to young men have moved to the White suburbs, away from the inner city, while clerical jobs, rapidly increasing and 80 percent female, are growing in downtown areas that are more accessible, both physically and psychologically, to inner-city residents. A major reason for the decline in male participation in the family is due to the change in the economy.

Many job counselors tell me that before we find these teenagers a job, we need to locate one for their parents. This book will continue to look at *Motivating and Preparing Black Youth For Success*, but I am not oblivious to the plight of Black adults. The major question is, what are half the Black teenagers who are unable to find employment going to do? Beyond the streets, radio and television, where can Willie channel his energy and intellect?

Thousands of unemployed teenagers are on the streets trying to find ways to survive. What's open to them is not always legal, much less approved by society. In a *Chicago Tribune* article, young men talked about life on the street corner.

5

The People:

Willie Cintron is twenty.

Pedro Perez is seventeen.

Robert Caldero, a friend of Willie and Pedro, is a project director for the American Friends Service Committee.

WILLIE: I've been unemployed for a year and a half. I worked at Playskool. I was laid off. I get money. I got my ways.

PEDRO: I've been out of work about a year. I've done some work for my cousin off and on by rehabilitating old buildings. But there ain't much of that work.

WILLIE: Other guys I know are pushing drugs. They stand on the corners and throw it (deal in drugs). If a person's got good stuff, the customers'll come from everywhere. That's why people try to get the best.

PEDRO: Or you can make it stealing. Stripping cars or just taking what's around, jewelry, that kind of thing. Also, dealers have money and they make good fences for stolen goods.

PEDRO: On summer days you can get pretty good business. Some guys make $500 or $600 a week. It depends on the drugs. And it depends on the area. A lot of it's marijuana. But, it's also cocaine and pills. The customers drive up in cars. They ride bikes. They walk up.

WILLIE: Everybody is out there doing it. You see maybe fifty guys in my community on the corner throwing it.

PEDRO: Where I grew up there were a lot of factories around there. If you quit one, you could have always gone to another and get a job. But nobody leaves a job anymore, no matter how bad it is.

WILLIE: All my friends are stealing or dealing. They look for jobs but they can't find them. It's better to work, because of the chance you're going to get caught if you deal or steal, but the only jobs you can get are the slave jobs. That's what they call them in the neighborhood. A slave job is one in which you do heavy labor for the minimum wage. The people say, "The guy's a fool. He could be dealing."

PEDRO: Also, guns are a very heavy industry. If you have a good connection for guns, you can really make money.

WILLIE: When gangs are building up, it's the number of weapons that count.

ROBERT: It's just like the arms race between countries.

PEDRO: I am out trying to find a job. I have a diploma. Willie doesn't. It makes no difference. They want experience and they want training.

WILLIE: Dealing drugs is like a job. The guys are not all hoggish. They take turns throwing. They watch each other's back when the other guy is throwing. Mostly all my friends are in jail for dealing.

PEDRO: There are people who don't ever get caught. I'd say it's fifty-fifty. I know a guy who has been caught twelve times. He spends three nights of the week in jail and the other four he is out dealing. Another dude never had to spend a night in jail. He goes through channels and he has connections.

ROBERT: What's out there is worse than I've ever seen it. There's more people on the street corners and they are there all day. They have nothing to do. They are divorced from the rest of the economy and from the rest of society. The biggest factor is unemployment. It's strange to see that world out there with guys getting up at 10 a.m. and drinking beer and staying out there all day and dealing or stealing or doing nothing.

PEDRO: We got to get something. That's why people turn to stealing and drugs.

ROBERT: The worse part is you see guys really go out there and try. You see guys at 7 and 7:30 a.m. hop on a bus maybe four days a week to go to the suburbs to try to find a job. On the average, I'd say it takes a year or a year and a half doing that to find a job. That long is not considered unusual at all.

WILLIE: People sleep in the Humboldt Park just to be first in line to get day labor work from an office there. It's worse than slave labor. The guy who owns the place gets $45 a day each for them. He pays them $25 a day and charges them each $2 for bus fare. How can you support a family on $23 a day? That's for the dogs.

ROBERT: People do make money selling drugs, but only a few of them. I now have gotten a house and car out of it. It's small time. Say, the ordinary street corner dealer really keeps at it and does not get busted, he makes maybe $12,000 a year. He has to live with the fear of being arrested or his supply drying up. Only a few guys make real bucks.[5]

I believe when a problem is incurred by a few it may be an individual concern, but when the problem affects larger numbers the issues may rest within the society. Sidney Wilhelm, in the classic, *Who Needs the Negro* states,

the Negro is caught in the jaws of a technological vise operating in accord with economic and racist motives of white America. The technological trend implemented in terms of economic incentives and racism points to what seems to be an inevitable dispensability for the Black race. Under preindustrial technology whites exploited the Negro as an economic commodity to be bought, sold, and traded in an agricultural economy; under industrial technology the Negro transformed into an economic serf complementing the economic incentives of Northern capitalists. In the past, it was incumbent upon white America to balance racial values against economic incentives. But with the introduction of automation, the necessity virtually disappears. White America hopes the Negro will accept its design and passively accept the fate of total isolation within the ghetto. The ghetto is the equivalent of the Indian reservation. Just as the people of one reservation were debauched with whiskey sold by white men, so the people of the other are ravaged by drugs.[6]

It is not my desire to be so depressing in a book designed to motivate Black youth, but I do believe that to solve the problems facing Black youth requires a better understanding of the relationships between racism and economics. The melting pot theory is applicable to immigrants who voluntarily left Europe with the sole objective of improving their station in life. African Americans were forced to relocate to America, and it was understood that it was not for a better life, but servitude. The economic reason for the journey was to work; racism "justified" why Blacks were chosen. Alvin Toffler's, *Third Wave*, explains the waves as agriculture, industrialism, and post-industrialism or automation. With each passing wave, white America had less economic need for Black labor, consequently racism is expressed more with disdain, and best described in Wilhelm's book titled, *Who Needs the Negro?*

I also believe the change in the economy has affected our motivation. Who determines our value? Who determines if we're needed?

Should Willie stay in bed because plantations and factories are closed and robots don't need him? Self-definition and self-esteem are the first step toward self-control and self-actualization.

Let's take a look at the typical parental view of the present generation's work ethic. I recently took a taxi from the airport to a convention site for a presentation and entered into a conversation with the Black driver. He told me he was sixty-one years old, had worked on various jobs for the past fifty-one years, and planned to retire within the next four years. He said both he and his wife are hard workers, but his youngest son of fifteen is downright lazy. "I don't know what's wrong with these children today. They got more opportunities than I ever had, and all I wanted to do was *make it easier for them than it was for me.*" How many times have you heard that classic statement? Adults really do not know why children do not possess their drive and work ethic. Youth add to this communication problem with phrases such as, "Whatever," "You know," "Straight up." Young people actually believe they have communicated with such jargon, and to their peer group they have succeeded. The future of the Black race may be dependent on bridging this communication gap.

I don't believe adults or youths exclusively can be faulted for their views. I like to consider myself an advocate for youth. I try to see the world from their perspective which requires listening, eye contact, and observing their mannerisms. Somewhere in "whatever, you know, straight up" are significant clues. I think youth are growing up too fast. The combination of diet, television, and the economy has caused havoc during the period labeled childhood.

The American diet has changed over the years for complex reasons including profit, urbanization, and convenience. Since 1930, little girls have started their menstrual cycle six months earlier for every decade. Young girls are now starting their menstrual cycle as early as eight years of age.[7] The major reason is the increased protein in the diet. Every mother in the animal kingdom has the appropriate milk for her offspring. Dogs feed their puppies, cats feed their kittens, cows feed their calves but humans, the most sophisticated animal, send their babies to another animal for milk. Cow's milk develops the body; breast milk develops the brain. The move away from breast milk and the continued rise in the consumption of red meat coupled with the dietary decline in green vegetables has accelerated the developmental growth in youth.

Television has also increased the maturation rate of children with

9

the overexposure of sophisticated information at earlier ages. Neil Postman in the *Disappearance of Childhood* remarks:

> Children have command over speech at the age of seven. The printing press created a new definition of adulthood, based on reading competence. In an oral world where information is disseminated more through television than the printed word, first literacy disappears. The second is that education disappears. The third is that shame disappears. And the fourth, as a consequence of the other three, is that childhood disappears. [8]

You now can see parents and children wearing the same clothes and going to the same entertainment places. Parents are often called by their first names and want to be their children's buddies. Many parents no longer know how an eight-year-old girl should wear her hair, or when a twelve-year-old boy should be inside the house. The economic incentive for the disappearance of childhood lies in the fact that consumers spend the most money between twenty and thirty years of age. Advertisers have created a buying teenage market.

Conversely, the complex economy has delayed the entrance of youth into the work force. Young people historically have been able to work on a farm or enter a factory between thirteen and seventeen years of age. Witness that in 1910, only 10 percent of the American populus received a high school diploma, in contrast to 1980 when 85 percent of European-Americans, 75 percent of all African-Americans, and 55 percent of all Hispanic-Americans graduated from high school. [9] Now, however, the economy has moved into the third wave, automation, and therefore fewer unskilled positions are available. As a result, children are now staying in school longer than ever before, not because they like school more, but because it is required.

It is ironic that the diet and television have accelerated their physical growth and maturation, the economy has delayed their entrance into the world of work, and schools are being used primarily as a holding station. I do not believe the problem lies exclusively with our youth. More fundamentally, I feel we do not know *what* to do with young people and rather than address this issue we give children a speech on how hard we worked delivering morning papers, walking miles to schools, stocking and clerking after school and being a provider before our eighteenth birthday. I challenge adults to ask themselves, if they were sixteen living in this present day,

Most children do not lack money, clothes or diversion, but they do lack the emotional security of stable, loving parents.

---

could they weave their way through dietary changes, television, automation along with the larger societal problems of drugs, moral decadence, low teacher expectations, and family instability?

I hope now both adults and youths are more open-minded about the complex circumstances affecting motivation and work, and will not blame one another. What has happened to the work ethic? Remember the classic parental statement, "They got more opportunities than I ever had, and all I wanted to do was make it *easier* for them than it was for me." The key word was *easier*; humans, unlike other parents of the animal world, often make children more dependent. I stated in *Countering the Conspiracy to Destroy Black Boys*, some mothers *raise* their daughters and *love* their sons. We have too many sons over twenty dependent on their parents in the animal kingdom. Nature documentaries illustrate how other parents in the animal kingdom push their offspring out to learn survival and developmental skills. We suffer from a two-edged sword: poverty and affluence — poverty of the things in life that give life substance and meaning; affluence in the material rewards and diversions that increasingly demand our time, planning and constant vigilance to acquire and maintain.

Children suffer from a new kind of neglect. They do not lack money to spend, clothes to wear (for the most part), or diversions to occupy them, but they do lack terribly in having within them the kind of emotional security only stable and loving parents can provide. According to some researchers, work values are generally transferred from parent to child, and are well developed by the fifth grade.[10]

What effects does it have on children's potential work ethic when their parents work away from home? What is different between lacking knowledge about what your parents do and not having a working parent, one who receives welfare? What effect does it have on the work ethic when parents are unable to find work or are not paid enough to afford child care? What effect does acknowledging the fact that drug pushers and garbage men make more than teachers? Studs Terkel, in his book *Working*, interviewed hundreds of workers in every conceivable occupation, and heard these comments regarding the work ethic:

> What a lot of young people rebel against is having to go into corporations where they have to spend thirty years of their lives and come out a wornout human being on a pension. The depression in the thirties was a unique period. People were willing to work and there wasn't work around. I think the mentality of the thirties and the mentality today is different. Then people really wanted to work. Now the thing is to want something *meaningful*: I didn't start out as president. It was necessary for me to scrub toilets. Not that I liked doing it. But I didn't feel debased by it. It was better than doing nothing. Any work is better than no work. Work makes a person noble. Another worker responds: Jobs are not big enough for people. It's not just the assembly line worker whose job is too small for his spirit. A job like mine, if you really put your spirit into it you would sabotage it immediately. You don't dare. So you absent your spirit from it. My mind has been so divorced from my job except as a source of income.[11]

A review of all major studies on work satisfaction concluded that there has been a significant decline in overall job satisfaction. The trend includes a shorter workday and week, flextime, more frequent vacations, early and better financed retirement, and greater interest in leisure. One of eight consumable dollars goes to recreation, and the industry nears 300 billion dollars annually.[12] Alvin Toffler in the *Third Wave* describes it very succinctly.

We must recognize three basic requirements of any individual: The needs for community, structure, and meaning. The complex changes in our society creating diversity caused feelings of loneliness. In the past economy, the structure resulted from the trio of home, school, and corporation, but with each year they have declined in their influence on youth. Ultimately, people are looking for a sense of purpose or meaning in their lives. The rising influence of "dogmatic" organizations or cults propose having the sole truth about life. The cult, however sells community, structure and meaning at an extremely high price. The mindless surrender of self. For many of course this price is too high, but the search for community, structure, and meaning continues.[13]

The first chapter in *Motivating and Preparing Black Youth For Success* has looked at "the politics of work." Willie represents many Black youth not operating at their full potential. The reasons are numerous, and include racism, low self-esteem, lack of concerned positive role models, and the changing economy from labor to capital-intensive. This change has made a large part of the population, and specifically Black youth, expendable. Large numbers of unmotivated Black youth turn to welfare and crime for survival. Segments of the Black talented tenth, many adults, and White media propagandists blame the victim for his plight without considering all pertinent factors. The issues may be that White America does not know what to do with Black people, and Black parents don't know what to do with their youth.

The work ethic has changed from 1619 and 1930 to the present. In order to motivate Black youth, we must go beyond understanding the economic, political, and social arena; and determine in the next chapter the role values play in motivation.

Deluged with new products, bombarded by advertising, and armed with credit cards, for many the motivation in life has become consumption.

Chapter 2

Values as the Foundation for Motivation

My two sons, thirteen and eight, are riding in the back seat of our four-year-old Volkswagen Rabbit. They are involved in one of their favorite games: "That's my car." The objective of the game is to be the first to point at the most desirable car; the favorites include sport cars and large automobiles, preferably limousines. In our home, I have taught them to play concentration, scrabble, boggle, checkers, cards and ball games, but neither I nor their mother taught them "that's my car." They did not formally or consciously learn this game from electronic or print media. Where did they learn it? Who taught them these values?

I recently spoke at an annual Black Men's conference. The analysis of the preceding year had determined that the number one problem facing Black men was unemployment. The solution appeared simple: provide employment for Black men and the major problem has been resolved. A change in government personnel could eradicate the problem, and, conversely, a subsequent change could restore the problem. I pondered if the plight of Black men and their masculinity rested on economic policies and governmental shifts. I wondered how a job determined if a Black man would stay with his children and help with their homework, moral and cultural lessons, and domestic responsibilities. I contemplated how Black women feel about their man when he receives a pink slip.

The headline in a major Chicago newspaper reads, "East Meets West — and Finds Decadence." Shown below it are two female Japanese teenagers, one wearing blue jeans and a Boy George tee-shirt, and the other wearing an above the knee length dress. Two months ago, at the peak of its popularity, the hit song "One Night in Bangkok," was banned by the Japanese government. Over the past two years, the average Japanese has increased in weight by fifteen pounds with the emergence of McDonald's, Kentucky Fried Chicken, and Shakey's Pizza.[1]

Values are the "invisible institution" says Richard Simmons in the *Crucial Element in The Development of Black Children,*[2] and they are so deeply ingrained that my sons, Black men, Asians and most of us never had a chance to determine our own values. The Purchasing Council reports that 60 percent of all supermarket purchases were not predetermined by the consumer, but were bought because of suggestive advertising. It becomes almost suicidal to enter a store without a list and a made-up mind to stick to it. Similarly, our values may also be largely determined by external pressures.

What make this subject and chapter so difficult is because values are often intangible. Most of us don't know why we do what we do or like what we like, but are convinced that whatever the reason, its ours and original. When I hear my sons enthusiastically claim their cars, I think of my possible responses. I could tell them to stop playing the game, but that would not eliminate the desire, change the values, nor prevent them from playing the game in my absence. I could make the game intellectual and raise technical questions concerning gas mileage, maintenance, durability, and costs. I could be emotionally disappointed that they don't value our car, or I could say nothing and think about what Eastern utilitarian value I could offer to compete against a Trans Am or a Mercedes. I don't have to leave my car to better understand the tremendous impact Western values have on youth. I actually believe I'm competing for the minds of my children and I'm pleased that I see it as competition rather than collaboration.

The challenge of providing alternative values is a very difficult task. Johari Amini comments:

> A value base is the foundation of every society. And as a consequence, desired changes in institutions or systems can take place only on a superficial level at best unless changes have first occurred in the value base of the society. Therefore, changing an imperialist exploitative peoples economic system from capitalism to socialism or communism will not retard or change their imperio-exploitative behavior; if the values of a society dictate that the people believe in competition, exploitation of others, and imperialism, those people will continue behaving in those ways, regardless of their economic system, until their society's value base itself is changed.[3]

I believe that Black men have something very valuable to offer their children regardless of their present employment status. When man got separated from the land and self-sufficiency and sold his labor into the marketplace, values, self-esteem, and sufficiency were predicated on money. Masculinity, marriage, and parenting for almost all men hinges on income. As Amini pointed out, it is difficult to change individual values beyond a superficial level without a societal change, but it is suicidal for us to allow our children to play "that's my car," for men to leave their family because they can't find work, and for Asian teenagers to forfeit their ancient rich tradition for the recent ideas of Madison and Fifth Avenue. Let's take a historical look at how society became inculcated with its present value system.

Quality	Southern Cradle (African)	Northern Cradle (European)
Descent	Matrilineal	Patrilineal
Gods	One Universal God	Familistia Gods
Social Philosophy	Collective, Xenophilic	Individualistic Xenophobic
Ancestor Worship	Burial	Cremation
Mode of Existence	Agrarian, Settled	Nomadic

Cheikh Anta Diop's two-cradle theory is based on three premises. Firstly, differences had to do with the climate and the specific conditions of life. Secondly, in passing from South to North, all cultural values were overthrown and became opposite as the poles. Ancient Africa was opposed to Europe in its conceptions of domestic life, state craft, philosophy, etc. Thirdly, the requirements of nomadic life and those of settled life provide all the elements of an explanation which makes it possible to clarify the subject. Diop's two-cradle theory links a matrilineal descent system (not matriarchy) to African agrarian life, and a patrilineal descent system (male supremacy) to European nomadic life.[4]

Please remember it was Europeans traveling into Africa not the reverse, and the major reason was the need for life-sustaining natural resources. Climate not only affected personalities historically, but I've noticed many people have a much more relaxed, giving disposition when the weather is warm rather than in arctic conditions. Secondly, paralleling Diop's analysis, secure people are comfortable with differences, they do not see opposite as being in conflict.

17

European	African
God vs. Man	God
Faith vs. intellect	Nature Family
Man vs. woman	Community
Color vs. non-color	

Thirdly, our agrarian lifestyle respected land, glorified home and family, and respected women and children. Our ability to survive the worst oppression ever placed on a people may well be attributed to these values, and in order to survive the present onslaught of value changes we should return to them.

Our objective is "motivating and preparing Black youth for success," but this is predicated on values. What are we motivating Black youth to work for? Money? Fame? Individualism? Do I motivate my sons with a Trans Am or a Mercedes? If not, how do I motivate them? When are they affected by society's present values? How did my sons begin to receive messages from the "invisible institution?"

Johari Amini provides the following model.

Values **Frame of Reference** **Motivation** **Behavior**

"There is no contradiction or inconsistency between what ones true beliefs or values are, and what one actually does. There are no contradictions, errors, or mistakes in behavior. We *act out what is in us*, nothing more, nothing less."[5]

I firmly believe that values and images don't lie. What a person says may be false, but what a person does and wears is consistent. How men treat their wives, mothers and sisters tell me more about how they feel toward Black women than what they say. What a person puts in his/her hair, on his/her face, and walls at home says more than words can describe.

The model provides four key stages: values, frame of reference, motivation and behavior. My objective is to motivate and prepare Black youth to work. If this is the desired result, a better understanding of values is necessary because of their impact on the latter three stages. I appeal to the reader to make this invisible institution of values as concrete as possible, either by reflecting on your own examples or that of my sons playing "that's my car."

Diop and Amini provided a historical/psychological analysis of values. Christopher Lasch in *Culture of Narcissism* offers a contemporary view.

To live for the moment is the prevailing passion — to live for yourself, not for your predecessor or posterity. We are quickly losing the sense of historical continuity, the sense of belonging to a succession of generations originating in the past and stretching into the future. A society that fears it has no future is not likely to give much attention to the needs of its children. Until recently, the Protestant work ethic stood as one of the most important underpinnings of American culture. According to the myth, thrift and industry held the key to material success and spiritual fulfillment. In an age of diminishing expectations these virtues no longer excite enthusiasm, in a simpler time advertising called attention to the product, now it manufactures a product of its own: The consumer perpetually unsatisfied, restless, anxious and bored. Advertising serves not so much to advertise products as to promote consumption as a way of life. The tired worker, instead of attempting to change the conditions of his work, seeks renewal in brightening his immediate surroundings with new goods and services.[6]

It is very difficult for a consumer, bombarded by a 70 billion dollar advertising industry and banks that conveniently offer credit cards, to resist purchasing. For many living in a self-centered society, bored with work or school, deluged with new products or old products with different shapes and colors, their motivation in life has become consumption. You need not be denied whatever your heart or their ads persuade you to purchase. I'm sure many of us have read about credit card abuse, but it should be obvious by the growth in installment purchases and bankruptcy, that it continues. I also am concerned with tempering the use of credit cards *before* insolvency has transpired. Credit cards are ideal as a substitute for cash or in lieu of a check in those institutions that do not accept them, but it should not be used to live above our means.

One day I was glancing through magazines and began critically looking at the advertisements. Black magazines are filled with alcohol, cigarette, and cosmetics ads. (Blacks are 13 percent of the population, earn only 6 percent of the income, but spend 39, 38 and 30 percent respectively in these areas.) I began cutting the ads out to show that what we purchase may be the result of sophisticated promotion. The first test case was my family. Right after dinner we had "Show and Tell." I showed the ads, but covered up the product name and asked then what was advertised. One ad was for cigarettes, but no one was smoking! There were two Black men and one woman having fun on a skateboard; the message was, smoking is as invigorating as exercising outdoors. Another ad was for liquor. A

Black couple are walking into a ballroom dressed in after-five attire. My children thought they were advertising clothes! The ad, not implicitly but explicitly, showed that drinking whiskey will make you look like a model. The last ad they never figured out. A very well-dressed, handsome, Black man is standing in the doorway. In front of him are two legs of a Black woman, the legs are spread apart forming a triangle effect, with the floor as the base. The three-dimensional effect has the man's head at the top of the triangle or in between the legs! What do you think was being advertised? A product? What type? The man's hair care? His clothes? Her stockings or shoes? Wrong. They were advertising cologne. In reality, they were advertising sex and values through "Night Musk."

I asked the boys, "How do television actors get paid? Do you put coins in the set in order to turn it on?" It took some time for them to appreciate the relationship between commercials and income for television owners and actors. Advertisers are confident enough in their ability to persuade, so they spend up to a half a million dollars on a thirty-second ad during the Super Bowl game, and expect a sizeable rate of return.

In this chapter on values, I'm looking at these relationships to motivating Black youth to work. What is it that we value? What do adults value? What do children value? Are the values of the adults different from youths? What is the purpose in life? I have learned through conducting workshops and teaching that people tend to provide what they think will be the right answer regardless of whether it's their answer. If I asked most people, "What is your purpose?" They would probably answer by saying, "To help somebody, to make the world better, to get closer to God." But if I asked them, "What do you spend most of your working hours doing, or what would you like to do with these hours?" I believe the responses would be, "Making money, shopping, feeling and looking good."

I asked young people if they had only one choice between money, house, car, clothes, land, and time, which would they choose? Many brothers choose cars. Many sisters choose clothes. Adults often prefer houses. Large numbers select money. But when I inquire, "What would you do with the money?" They respond with, "Buy a house, car, and clothes." Very few choose land. Yet it is the only commodity that can't be made in a factory, and it's the source of our food, clothing, and shelter. Even fewer choose time, and many chose it because they felt it's the "right answer," not because they value it. Returning to Amini's model, our behavior doesn't indicate that we value time more than money, cars, clothes and houses. Many of us give our time to soap operas, gossiping, and street life, but will fight and kill over the mistreatment of our money, cars, clothes and houses.

There are many adults who do not like their work, but love money and what it will buy. The term "TGIF" (Thank God it's Friday) illustrates that large numbers of people are dissatisfied with how they spend the largest part of their week and life, consequently use the shortest part to pacify a dying spirit. The average adult spends eight hours working a job he doesn't like. They spend two hours for transportation, three hours for breakfast, lunch, dinner and their preparation. This total of thirteen hours, plus eight hours sleeping leaves three hours for recreation. Many adults dislike Monday through Friday, but enjoy weekends. Some adults do not like what they do from ages twenty-one to sixty-five, and look forward to enjoying life upon retirement. I believe a strong motivation would be finding enjoyment during the longest period of your life.

I have been accused of being too critical and over-simplifying the above scenario. But if you tell me you value time more than anything else, as Amini's model points out, "then the truth ain't in it." I would admit, though, that if you're thirty-five years or older, have a spouse and children, and are over-committed in debt and living from paycheck to paycheck it is difficult to quit a job you don't like, return to school or start the business you've often thought about. Going back to school or starting your business doesn't pay the salary in the first year your present lifestyle requires.

My father made sure I didn't work with him in the post office. He told me he saw talented youth work there while in school and enjoyed making a good income, often one that would surpass many "degreed" professions. Many of them dropped out of school, continued to work for money rather than personal satisfaction, and started their merry journey to "over-extended city and bankruptcy USA."

I believe people value time, but a synonym for values is priorities. A value or priority is more significant when placed within the context of choices. Behavior, not words, is the best indication of values. For many of us when forced to choose, prioritize between money and time, value money. The University of Michigan conducted a survey in 1950 and repeated it in 1980 to determine the major influences on children. Listed below are its findings.

1950	1980
1) home	1) home
2) school	2) peers
3) church	3) television
4) peers	4) school
5) television	5) church[7]

If we accept the position that values determine behavior and values are a result of exposure to information, then suffice to say whoever controls print and electronic media will have a lot to say about values. What institutions teach youth to value time? What institutions or advertisements teach youth the difference between needs and wants? Who will teach youth the value of savings? I believe this is the responsibility of parents and educators — and it starts by example. It is very difficult to teach children when our behavior is in direct contradiction to our professed values. I encourage us to manage our time better than we do our check books. I recommend that we develop a time chart for the day and allocate the appropriate time for each task. I've often pondered that many of our talented people made their invention, record or contribution to society while the rest of the populace was watching television, talking on the telephone or hanging on the streets. These "gifted" stars may be ordinary people, but they used their time like a gift.

I also suggest that we equip children with an "advertising defense" to the avalanche of promotion directed at them. Youth should be taught the difference between needs and wants. When children are watching commercials, parents should quiz them on which is which. For example, designer jeans are a want, while regular jeans may be a need if your wardrobe warrants it. This game can also be played in the grocery store. They can put needs in the basket, but not wants. As mentioned earlier with magazine ads, we should ask what is being advertised? A product? Exercise? Good looks? Sex?

We should also teach our children the significance of savings. Many view savings as anything leftover after we've gone shopping. As a result, very little if anything ever ends up in savings. To insure that savings receives its share, I recommend savings be allocated *before* not *after* consumption. My wife and I give our children an allowance of which a certain percentage is for savings, and if they allow it to grow throughout the year, then at the end we will provide a "matching grant." We have found this not only encourages savings, but teaches them how savings can become an investment. (More will be said about investment in the concluding chapter.)

As Johari Amini pointed out, values of the individual are difficult to change if the values of the society remain the same.

African	Euro-American
We	I
Cooperation	Competition
Internal	External

Maulana Karenga in *The Theory of Kawaida* offers the Nguzo Saba.

UMOJA (Unity)
To strive for and maintain unity in the family, community, nation and race.

KUJICHAGULIA (Self-determination)
To define ourselves, name ourselves, create for ourselves and speak for ourselves instead of being defined, named, created for and spoken for by others.

UJIMA (Collective Work and Responsibility)
To build and maintain our community together and make our sister's and brother's problems our problems, and to solve them together.

UJAMAA (Cooperative Economics)
To build and maintain our own stores, shops and other business, and to profit from them together.

NIA (Purpose)
To make our collective vocation the building and developing of our community in order to restore our people to their traditional greatness.

KUUMBA (Creativity)
To do always as much as we can, in the way we can, in order to leave our community more beautiful and beneficial than we inherited it.

IMANI (Faith)
To believe with all our heart in our people, our parents, our teachers, our leaders and the righteousness and victory of our struggle.[8]

Val Jordan offers *The Black Value System*.

Commitment to God
Commitment to the Black community
Commitment to the Black family
Dedication to the pursuit of education

Dedication to the pursuit of excellence
Adherence to the Black work ethic
Commitment to self-discipline and self-respect
Disavowal of the pursuit of middle classness[9]

Karenga's and Jordan's value systems are positive contributions in our quest to reorder our society. Many homes, schools, churches, and other institutions teach their youth and members these values. Unfortunately, many times these positive values have been memorized and regurgitated in rote fashion. The first step is for these values to be given to youth, but the next step is their internalization. We need youths and adults who will depict in their behavior a commitment to God, the Black community, family, education, excellence, work ethic, and self-discipline.

In a society obsessed with self-preservation and "what's in it for me" there are few advertisements promoting unity, self-determination, collective work and responsibility, cooperative economics, purpose, creativity and faith.

We have to select books for children that encourage sharing and being your brother's keeper. Family rituals ranging from having dinner together, cleaning together, and being considerate when there is only one glass of juice left and two people want it. This reminded me of a church retreat I went on where we talked all day about sharing with one another. At dinner, shrimp was served and "sharing Christians" became selfish animals fighting over an inadequate amount of shrimp for the group. In contrast, at the same retreat a little girl was told to pass out candy to the group. She was one piece short and an adult still needed candy. She pondered her options, gave the lady her candy and smiled.

I acknowledge Amini's respect for the values of the dominant society, but if she did not think they could be changed, she never would have written her article, Karenga and Jordan would not have created their value system, and I would not be thinking of strategies to counter "that's my car." And I would not appeal to youth to value time over money. *I do not believe we can motivate Black youth for success if the highest value in life is to make money.* I believe our youth have found other ways to make money besides working hard and receiving a "good education." I strongly suggest a change of our values from money to time, from materialism to the Nguzo Saba and the Black Value System. The next two chapters on motivation and talent, begin to offer alternatives to our present value system.

Chapter 3

Motivation For Success

Rick and Anthony's two young brothers are too excited to fall asleep. For the past hour their parents have told them that if they don't get any rest they will be sleeping in school. Rick and Anthony are so eager to go to school they can't sleep. This will be Anthony's first year, and he's heard from his brother, who is a "one year veteran," how great it is to be in school. Rick says, "There are more children in school than in the whole wide world. We sing songs, color, listen to stories, play at recess, and eat lunch. They even give you papers to do at home. I like to do mine as soon as I eat my snack. I really like school."

Leon and Kathy, two high school students, are sitting in the park "shooting the breeze," during their seventh-period class. They've been friends since sixth grade which was four years ago. They checked into their "home room" between third and fourth period to be officially in attendance. Unofficially, they've been talking, eating, smoking reefer, and drinking beer for the last three periods in the park. Leon's says, "School is a drag and all I want is some paper to enlist in the Army." Kathy knows the three classes she missed base their grades on a mid-term and a final exam. She has friends with copies of the exams, so there is no need to attend or study.

What happened between kindergarten and tenth grade to the eagerness and enthusiasm to learn? Were Leon and Kathy always that way? Did they ever feel like Rick and Anthony? Will Rick and Anthony feel like Leon and Kathy when they become teenagers? In one of my earlier books, *Countering the Conspiracy to Destroy Black Boys*, one chapter is called "The Fourth Grade Failure Syndrome." Research showed a decline in academic achievement with age, which probably paralleled their enthusiasm.[1]

Our children are bored; adolescence isn't a training ground for adulthood, it is a holding pattern for aging youth.

Harry Morgan says: "When Blacks enter first grade, the stories they create express positive feelings about themselves in the schooling situation, but by the second grade their stories express negative imagery of the teacher and school environment and by the fifth grade, the overall feeling expressed by students is that of criticism. In other words, upon entering school in primary grades, Black children possess enthusiasm and eager interest, however, by fifth grade, the liveliness and interest are gone, replaced by passivity and apathy. Primary grades presented a more nurturing environment than intermediate or upper grades. In early childhood education, much of the activity is child-teacher centered and a great deal of interaction between children. The classroom environment in the upper grades is transformed from a socially interactive style to a competitive individualistic and minimally socially interactive style of learning."[2]

The drop-out rate has reached epidemic levels ranging from 23 percent nationally to 49 and 55 percent respectively in the Black and Brown communities.[3] A table of Chicago Public High Schools illustrates the plight.

Percentage of freshmen tested who read
at or above the national average:

Lane	88	Westinghouse	17
Young	83	Fenger	15
Lindblom	74	Harlan	14
Von Steuben	66	Bowen	14
Kenwood	63	Clemente	14
Lincoln Park	49	Gage Park	14
Mather	49	Hirsch	14
Taft	45	Corliss	14
Morgan Park	43	Richards	13
Prosser	41	Carver	13
Curie	40	Near North	13
Metro	39	Kelvyn Park	13
Washington	37	Wells	13
Bogan	37	South Shore	13
Hyde Park	33	Crane	9
Steinmetz	33	Farragut	9
Kennedy	30	King	9
Amundsen	28	Tilden	7
Roosevelt	26	Robeson	7
Dunbar	27	Marshall	7
Hubbard	24	Manley	7
Julian	24	Collins	6
Juarez	24	Austin	6
C.V.S.	23	DuSable	6
Schurz	22	Calumet	5
Foreman	22	Flower	5
Simeon	22	Harper	5
Senn	21	Cregier	5
Kelly	20	Phillips	5
Sullivan	17	Orr	4[4]

Chicago schools are not the exception, but the norm. Each year schools receive students like Rick and Anthony, and we must prevent them from becoming like Leon and Kathy. High school teachers cite the lack of motivation as their number one problem. Students drop out for this reason, as well as poor grades, student-teacher incompatibility, economics, and pregnancy.[5] A decade ago the adults and the college crowd were the principal users of marijuana. Then it became the high school crowd, until it started experimenting with speed pills and cocaine. More recently, the big growth in marijuana use has been among the junior-high crowd. A common reason given for the upsurge in drug use by youngsters is boredom.[6]

Our children are bored, and this is expressed in their slang when they say, "whatever," "you know," and "straight up." In an earlier chapter, I mentioned the terrible trick that has been played on them. The combination of accelerated physical maturation coupled with overexposure to electronic media has produced youth unable to accept their invisible role in the "Third Wave Economy" of automation.

I believe youths have a story to tell if adults will listen. When I ask youth, "What do your parents and teacher tell you about school?" The youth respond with, "Get a good education and work hard." When I ask them how they feel about those comments, they answer, "Get a good education for *what*? Work hard for *who*?" The youth also want to know the relevancy, need or reason why for each lesson.

Youth observe adults with their "good education" and they wonder what adults end up with. A j-o-b which they don't like, consequently, they end up living for "TGIF" (Thank God It's Friday). Youths quickly conclude that life is about money, not a good education or a job. They also wonder, "If working hard is the solution, why aren't Black people more advanced since Blacks were brought here to work?" I believe adults have not been honest with youth. Have you ever thought about the inverse relationship between age and asking questions, or the direct relationship between age and cheating? Rick and Anthony entered school assuming the learning experience would be shared between students and teachers, so they asked all kinds of questions. Why is it that Leon and Kathy don't ask as many questions as they did in the primary grades? Do you think Rick and Anthony would cheat on a test given the first day of school? When would they begin to cheat? Why? Do you think Leon and Kathy cheat? When did they start?

I believe our youth stopped asking questions and began cheating when they found out the most important objective in school was not learning, but receiving good *grades*. I further postulate our youth have determined that securing employment is based more on *who* you know than *what* you know. I do not believe you can motivate and prepare Black youth with a lie.

If the objective in life is to make money, our youths see numerous ways to achieve this without a "good education or working hard." If we encourage a good education and working hard, the motive will have to be something other than money. How can adults — specifically educators — promote learning without simultaneously insisting on more questions? Many adults view education (degrees) as a plateau rather than a process. The first and probably greatest university, The Grand Lodge of Wa'at in Egypt, admitted students at the age of seven, and studies were not completed until forty years later! Many contemporary educators become masters and doctors much earlier and stop learning.

I agree our youth do need to work hard and receive a good education, but do the same parents who advocate this know the distinction between being educated and being trained? The latter is a very passive experience and an exercise in information regurgitation while the former is active, challenging, relevant, and encourages youth to be inquisitive.

Working hard has always been an admirable goal, slaves did not slow down because they were lazy, but because they were not the beneficiaries of their labor. Employers opt to work longer far more often than employees who require overtime compensation in contrast to owners who do it for long-term growth. Parents have always found dirt in the house that their children didn't see, one reason being pride in ownership was more instilled in the parents. Parents reinforce this view by saying, "You don't do that in *my* house!" The desire to work hard has to be connected to benefits and goals. Students work harder when they see the relationship between theory and practice, a more hands-on experience. Black youth, and specifically Black male youth, literally demand to see the connection between the classroom and the streets.

Black adults may know that schools value grades more than learning, and employers reply more to referrals than credentials, but they do not know anything else to tell Black youth other than to work hard and get a good education. Very few Black adults equip Black youth with a sense of cultural and racial pride, so that when they see racism, they don't view *themselves* as inferior, but view the *discriminator* as having an insecurity problem. Even fewer Black adults encourage their youth to start their own business. The combination of mass public school education geared toward manufacturing employees, and parents not instilling pride to be the boss creates frustration for Black youth. Almost half the Black youth drop out, and the other half who believed a good education would

make them the chief executive officer of a "Fortune 500" corporation, now bitterly accept the reality that they can only go so far in
someone else's corporation.

Our objective is to motivate Black youth to work. Parents, peers
and media may motivate them to consume, but that doesn't always
create a burning desire to work hard and receive a good education.
Our youth today often desire a $200,000 lifestyle but possess only
five-dollar skills. Youth tell me they're going to *be* a doctor, lawyer,
or engineer, but when I ask about their progress in math, reading,
and science they give lackadaisical responses. Youths say, "I'm
going to *be* Michael Jordan or Whitney Houston," without an
appreciation of what it requires to *become* anything.

Youth are motivated to *be* great, but not motivated to *become*
great which requires discipline, time management, vision, patience,
and, above all else, work. This misconception of the rigors involved
are best attributed to youth watching "instant success" stories on
television, and not observing how their parents earn a living. When
I ask youth what kind of lifestyle they want, their answer includes a
large house, a two-car garage with, of course, two luxury cars, fine
clothes and appliances, and the money to travel. I then ask what
kind of career will pay for it and what are its requirements? The
answers are not forthcoming. Somehow youth feel they can skate
from kindergarten to twelfth grade then accelerate, bloom and
blossom in college.

I again do not fault our youth. I believe they are the product of
their experiences. Earlier, I mentioned the terrible trick that has
been played on youth via the diet, media, and the economy. I believe
adults do not know what to do with youth. Today, school is what
young people do for a living. While a high school diploma or a college
degree no longer guarantees a job, there are more jobs you can't
even apply for without them. So the payoff is less certain, but the
pressure is even greater to go to school longer and longer, to extend
the state of semi-autonomy further and further.

The irony is that society worries more when the young try to
grasp at adult "privileges" than when they remain in the passive
fraternity-house state of mind. We worry about teenage drinking
and driving and pregnancy — all perhaps misguided attempts at
"grown-up behavior." School just isn't enough. It demands only
certain skills, tests only for certain concepts. Adolescence isn't a
training ground for adulthood now, it is a holding pattern for aging
youth.

Many adults respond to this dilemma with advice from the "good old days" — days filled with two parents, of which only one worked; little to no television; music void of "I Wanna Sex You Up" and "Pop That Coochie"; a reverence for teachers, an extended-family neighborhood where every child could be disciplined by an adult, and a church-going community. I respect and encourage adults who want to maintain a more "traditional" lifestyle, but I have concerns when adults give "traditional" advice without providing a "traditional" home, school, and church environment which monitors the peer group and television. Adults need to give advice which includes the *present* reality youths find themselves.

I often challenge adults by asking, "If you were a teenager could you weave your way through what they have to endure?" I want to focus briefly on the peer group; presently it has the second greatest influence nationally on youth, after the home and before television. Why? The peer group has more time. The declining hours from the home have been divided between peer group and television — and the peer group reinforces much of what is seen on television.

Many parents have become very liberal and passive in rearing their children. While the problems of inadequate time and not listening to their children should be obvious, the subtle mistake is not sharing their perspective on contemporary issues. What was our analysis when our youths saw "Purple Rain" or any television show, movie, video, or commercial? What was our opinion when educational and developmental programs solicited their attendance? How are youths going to understand our position on anything if they do not work with us, and we do not communicate with them when we arrive home? In the movie "Purple Rain," there was a scene where Prince drove Appolonia (the leading actress) to the lake, and talked her into undressing. What was your position with your son and/or daughter?

I am involved with several youth programs. The major reason for their creation was to provide viable options to our youth, but I learned to realize that the problem often is not the lack of community programs but their sparse attendance due to parents allowing teenagers to decide if they should attend Bible study, piano lessons, academic tutoring and cultural awareness sessions or staying home on Saturday morning watching videos or playing basketball. Adults need to push their values, if for no other reason than that the peer group and media will push theirs.

We offer few alternatives, few meaningful opportunities for

adulthood training. We have virtually allowed sex, drinking, and driving to become rites of passage. Without enough alternatives, schools are left to produce adults, but schools are where the young are kept, not where they grow up.

Listed below are some alternatives for young people:
1) Volunteer in a blue-collar field to learn skills such as carpentry, electricity, and plumbing.
2) Manage the family budget and do the grocery shopping.
3) Volunteer to work for a firm to learn about word processing and computers.
4) Join the school newspaper and learn writing, editing, and graphic design.
5) Learn maintenance of the family car.
6) Volunteer for work with an investment firm to learn the stock market.
7) Join a science club.
8) Learn to play a musical instrument.
9) Improve your personality, communication skills, and income by selling a product.
10) Visit the sick in hospitals.

I have read numerous articles describing the plight of youth and the ambivalence of adolescence. Many writers advocate the need for such alternatives as the above. The assumption is based on the notion that our youth are bored and feel unproductive, therefore, by providing these alternatives and more, we can motivate them. Wrong! When I gave youth an option to choose the above or eat pizza and watch videos, they chose the latter in every case. These options can only be useful if we encourage and/or demand their participation.

In conclusion, our children did not come to us bored, but teacher pedagogy, parental dishonesty or ambiguity about how to "make it" in America, have left youth asking fewer questions, cheating on tests, and dropping out of school. I believe we are not going to motivate youth without being honest, sensitive to the present reality, and assertive in our views. I strongly encourage the use of the alternatives provided to make adolescents more productive, but it might require adults mandating their participation.

I also believe that an appreciation of African American history can motivate youth. I did not say Negro history which is taught only in February, memorizing names and dates, or allocating one week each to Africa and the middle passage, and the remaining weeks of the course to America. Many youths are ashamed of Africa and slavery. A historian or a teacher decides *before* they write or teach where they want the reader or student to be upon completion. When we teach African American history do we want to make the students docile and ashamed or assertive and proud? Our youths have a right to know how a people so great went from pyramids to projects. I strongly feel that a committed teacher or parent can motivate our youths with the African American experience. We were a great people and we withstood the greatest oppression ever placed on a people. In whatever industry or occupation we've been "permitted" to enter we have excelled. We must teach our youth their history and potential. We must use racial pride to motivate them to become the best they can be.

Lastly, I believe the best way to motivate Black youth is not with money, but through the development of their God-given talents. The next chapter will look at how these talents can be identified, developed, and used for motivation.

Children have innate ability, potential and intellect, the full development of which is dependent upon opportunities and encouragement.

Chapter 4

The Development of Talents into a Career

From the book of Matthew:

And unto one he gave five talents, to another two, and to another, one to every man according to his ability. Then he that had received the five talents went and traded with the same, and made them five other talents. And likewise he that had received two, he also gained another two. But he that had received one went and digged in the earth, and hid his Lord's talent. After a long time the Lord of those servants cometh, and reckoneth with them. And so he that had received five talents came and brought other five talents, saying Lord, thou deliveredst unto me five talents: behold I have gained beside them five talents more. His Lord said unto him, well done, thou good and faithful servant: thou hast been faithful over a few things, I will make thee ruler over many things: enter thou into the joy of the Lord. He also that had received two talents came and said, Lord, thou deliveredst unto me two talents: behold, I have gained two other talents beside them. His Lord said unto him, well done, good and faithful servant. Then he which had received the one talent came and said Lord I was afraid, and went and hid thy talent in the earth. The Lord said take therefore the talent from him and give it unto him which hath ten talents. For to whom much is given, much is required.[1]

God has given all of us talents, but as the Scripture explains, if you don't *use* them, you will *lose* them. Recognizing your talents should provoke humility and responsibility. When you acknowledge that your gifts come from God, it should make you humble, but it should also encourage you to develop them. Let me offer three brief profiles for illumination: Paul Robeson, **Magic Johnson,** and **Jeremiah Wright.**

Paul Robeson was a star football, baseball and basketball player; a Phi Beta Kappa student who delivered the senior commencement address at Rutgers; a prolific singer of over 300 recorded songs; and a brilliant actor performing on stages internationally, all coupled with a law degree from Columbia University.

Earvin "Magic" Johnson has played for the Los Angeles Lakers since 1979. He has been the game's premier point guard leading the Los Angeles Lakers to five NBA titles. Three times he was named NBA's Most Valuable Player. He dazzled everyone with his championship season at Michigan State and his recent triumphs in the 1992 All-Star Game and "Dream Team" at the Summer Olympics in Barcelona. He is a major spokesman in educating youth about Aids-related issues and he now heads the Magic Johnson Foundation for Aids research.

Dr. Jeremiah Wright is pastor of Trinity United Church of Christ, one of the fastest growing congregations in America. His degrees range from the social sciences to theology, he speaks four different languages, he writes music, sings, and plays four different instruments, and serves on numerous boards of distinction. He was a cardio-pulmonary technician in the Navy and is actively involved in Trans-Africa and other African liberation movements. A friend of mine, Eugene Winslow, brilliant in his own right, has coined the phrase "use yourself up." Many people go all of their lives unfulfilled and continuously searching for happiness and contentment. Advertisements steer them to cars, clothes, houses, sex, drugs, and exotic resorts, but the pursuit continues. Our youth will take that same journey unless we have adults who will encourage them to look within, to "use themselves up." In the previous chapter on motivation, I declared money may not be adequate to inspire all youth to work hard and get a good education. I propose that in order to motivate youth to study and work they should be required to "use themselves up." The major purpose in life should be the exploration and development of all ones talents. Robeson, Johnson, and Wright are three fine examples of people who were given certain talents, but have added and multiplied them into many more.

I believe God has given *all* children talents and this chapter will explore how they can be developed and used for motivation. Unfortunately, when most people think of talents, what comes to mind are persons with extraordinary gifts and abilities. Even worse are Blacks who think of talents primarily in sports and music. Most would accept that Michael Jordan and Michael Jackson are talented, but do not conceive all children as being talented.

Benjamin Bloom comments in *Developing Talent in Young People*,

> After forty years of intensive research, my major conclusion is: What any person in the world can learn, 95% can also if provided with the appropriate conditions. (The remaining 5% is divided among the 2-3% with impairments and the 1-2% with exceptional learning skills.) By talent we mean an unusually high level of demonstrated ability, achievement, or skill in some special field of study or interest. This is in contrast with earlier definitions, which equate talent with natural gifts or aptitudes. This study has provided strong evidence that no matter what the initial characteristics (or gifts) of the individuals, unless there is a long and intensive process of encouragement, nurturance, education, and training, the individuals will not attain extreme levels of capability in these particular fields.[2]

I support Bloom's premise that children have innate ability, potential, aptitude, and talent; and its development is dependent on its nurturance. Bloom cites parental involvement, teachers, and the surrounding environment as key factors in talent development. The research examined the backgrounds of world-class performers in concert piano, sculpture, swimming, tennis and mathematical and neurological research. Parents were instrumental in their children's development by providing them time, money, the work ethic, and commitment. It was also noticed that children selected areas in which their parents had previously demonstrated interest and/or skill. Children did not necessarily choose the exact instrument or sport, but if their parents were musically or athletically inclined it was a catalyst for their child's decision. Income was needed for special tutors, teachers, and programs for talent enhancement. Teacher selection was critical because each stage of talent development requires a certain type of mentor. Lastly, the home, siblings, peers, and the larger community sanctioned and supported the endeavor.

From a Black perspective there is much extrapolation necessary to fully appreciate the study. The full development of talents is dependent on the extent to which there are opportunities and encouragement for individuals to find meaning and enjoyment. Blacks are talented in music and sports because of innate ability coupled with a society that encourages this form of expression. Jackie Robinson was "our first accepted," Henry Aaron hit the most homers, and Ricky Henderson stole the most bases, but don't you believe they had the most baseball talent in the history of our race. Blacks in Africa and America before the 1950s simply were denied the opportunity to express baseball talent. It does not mean they didn't have talents, but the environment was not conducive.

If a major incentive for being a concert pianist, sculptor, swimmer, tennis player, or researcher is dependent on parental interest and accomplishment, it could explain the limited scope to which many Blacks confine their talents. Blacks may be more talented in basketball, football, baseball, boxing and track than in swimming, tennis, bowling, golf and hockey because the former require less money and are supported by their peers. The large number of men who spend their evenings as baseball and basketball coaches, and churches who will teach singing in the choirs may help explain our excellence; and the lack of men and women who provide coaching in math, science, and debate programs may explain our detriment in these areas.

Jeff Howard and Ray Hammond from the Efficacy Committee commented in an article titled "Black America and the Psychology of Performance:"

> Important as the reality of racism may be in understanding the origins of our present problems, we believe our tendency to avoid intellectual engagement and competition limits our potential for development and progress. We contend that avoidance is rooted in reactions of fear and self-doubt engendered by strong negative stereotypes. Competition spurs development. The willingness to engage in competitive activity with commitment to high standards and success stimulates the discipline and effort that underlie intellectual development.[3]

The NAACP has done a fine job with the Academic Olympics, but we need far more. Where are the schools that will give more glory to their scholars than their athletes? That will give pep rallies, medals and trophies to the winners of debate, math, spelling, and science competitions. Young people see schools give more glory and employers give more money to ballplayers than to academicians. Our youth are motivated to make money, play ball, and sing, but we have not provided the support system for the development of other talents.

God has given "talents" to the entire human body. Many educators are familiar with the "split-brain theory." The brain is divided into two apparently symmetrical parts. The left side of the brain is analytical, divides things into sections and specializes in the functions of math and science. The right hemisphere is more holistic, relational, and appreciates the areas of music, art, dance, and sports. It has been rumored that men are better on the left and women better on the right. It has also been felt that people with greater levels of melanin are better on the right, and people with lower levels are better on the left. Are these theories accurate? Did God go to sleep with men on the right and wake up on the left? Did God wake up for Blacks on the right and fall back asleep on the left?

Is the above phenomenon nature (physical) or nurture (environment)? What can explain the tremendous rhythm of Black people and 86 percent of the starting players on NBA teams being Black, yet comprising only 1 percent of the engineers? Consider the following: If you practice dancing and playing basketball six hours daily after school, and spend little time in the library or laboratory, chances are you'll be a better dancer than dentist. If Black parents and teachers emphasize one style of learning over another or are afraid of math and science, this will have implications on the child's development. For example, teachers may offer 100 points for extra reading, 75 points for writing a research paper, but only 10 points for an original drawing. The large number of "degreed" people who can only draw on a primary level is appalling.

Talents are like hidden gifts dispersed throughout the body. It takes time and nurturance to identify and develop them all. Listed below is a miniature diagram.

Body	Characteristic	Possible careers
Right-brain	intuitive, holistic, visual	music/art/writing
Left- brain	logical, analytical	doctor/engineer accountant
mouth	good communication skill, extrovert	sales/media/ singer
hands	good dexterity	sewing/mechanics carpentry
larger body muscles	eye-hand coordination, graceful, strength, speed	athlete/dancer
heart	good listener, compassionate	minister/social worker/teacher
ego	leader	manager/ administrator

My major objective in this chapter is to change the concept that talents are only held by a few, and that Blacks only have talents for playing ball and musical entertainment. I would like to see parents, schools, and churches look at all children very early and provide them with numerous opportunities to develop their talents. One of the popular manuals used by guidance counselors is the *Self Directed Search*. First, it assumes that people can be loosely classified into six different groups: realistic, investigative, artistic, social, enterprising, and conventional. Some of the major characteristics of each group are as follows:

Realistic	Persistent, mechanical
Investigative	Critical, curious, independent, precise, good memory
Artistic	Original, imaginative
Social	Communicative, convincing, friendly
Enterprising	Adventurous, ambitious, domineering, efficient, orderly
Conventional	Efficient, orderly

I believe a major parental responsibility is to identify and develop children's talents. I also encourage adults who still do not know their children's talents to explore their possibilities. Reviewing the last two diagrams, the following characteristics were provided:

intuitive	holistic	visual
logical	analytical	communicative
extroverted	dexterous	graceful
speed	strength	eye-hand coordination
listening	leadership	persistent
mechanical	critical	curious
independent	good memory	precise
original	imaginative	compassionate
convincing	friendly	adventurous
ambitious	domineering	efficient
orderly		

I'm recommending that parents look at their children for all these characteristics (talents) and provide them with opportunities for major further enrichment. Bloom's study showed that parents were the major catalyst. One of the major obstacles for Black parents is the cost involved in talent development. The magazine, *Black Enterprise* featured an article, "Everything You'd Like to Give Your Kids But Weren't Sure You Could Afford." The article was a cursory look at the cost nationwide for various lessons in piano, drama, computers, and tennis. The average cost was *ten dollars per half-hour*, and, of course, to maximize instruction, each instructor encouraged the purchase of the equipment to practice at home.[5] Many Black parents don't have the advantages included in the demographics of the *Black Enterprise* subscriber — income, education, assets, etc. — consequently would have difficulty paying those fees. This further explains the perception that violin and tennis lessons are for the more well-to-do, and the excellence demonstrated by Blacks in basketball and singing is due to the combination of natural talent and free access to the means of developing these talents. The article, as an afterthought, mentioned the use of the Y. I further suggest the park district, day and evening schools.

My major recommendation in this area would be the Black church. The church has often been criticized for being open only on Sundays, and closed the rest of the week. The church should solicit from members talented instructors in math, science, writing, carpentry, electronics, sewing, speech, music, and sports, etc. These instructors could provide lessons to youth for much less than the cost cited in the article of ten dollars per half-hour.

The four factors preventing our youth from developing their talents are lack of adult identification, institutions, cost, and time. I have already addressed the first three; let's take a closer look at the obstacles of time. Much of the hyperactivity demonstrated by children can be attributed to diet and television. Today's generation of children are uncomfortable with "free time." They are either outside playing or watching television. If parents monitored television and often told them to turn it off, many children would say, "There is nothing to do and I'm bored." What they mean is "There is nothing to watch on television, and I don't know *how* to do anything." Boredom does not come from the *outside* in but the *inside* out. The African term is *inner*attainment, where there is no separation between performer and audience, when the drummer plays, the people dance. The European term is *enter*tainment, best illustrated at the opera where there is not only a distinct separation, but the audience only claps at designated intervals.

How could children filled with talents all over the body and abundant amounts of energy be bored? Besides the obvious fact that watching television takes vital time away from talent development, most children and adults do not have *hobbies*. Webster's Dictionary defines hobbies as "a favorite occupation or something pursued for amusement." I make a distinction between job and career. Jobs are something we have to do for income. Careers are like hobbies, they are a favorite occupation, something pursued for amusement. Can you imagine being paid for something you enjoy so much that you would do it for free, but because you do it so well, you get paid?

The merging of hobbies and talents should be a parental goal in children's development. I don't believe Paul Robeson, Magic Johnson, and Jeremiah Wright are exceptional or geniuses; I believe they just made the best use of their time to develop their talents.

I believe many of the great contributions of our day could have been made by a number of people if they had reduced their television viewing and other time wasters. This book is being written while some of my peers watch television, gossip on the telephone, and hang out on the streets. Children need hobbies for their free time. Listed below is a partial list of hobbies.

> animals: care, hunting, fishing
> baking: cooking
> carpentry
> collections: cards, coins, stamps
> dance
> drawing: painting, design
> electronics
> games: chess, checkers, Scrabble, etc.
> gardening
> musical instrument
> photography
> reading
> sculpture
> sewing
> singing
> sports
> travel: geography
> writing

Please note I did not mention watching television and listening to music. These are passive (entertainment) experiences. You develop very few little talents watching and listening to electronic media.

This may explain why our youth participate in Michael Jackson and Prince look-alike contests rather than being original. It is very difficult to be bored if you participate in several hobbies.

There is a thin line between achievers and underachievers. A popular statement teachers make to parents at conferences is, "He has the ability, but he's not using it." This statement lets most teachers and parents off the hook and places the weight on the youth for not maximizing his potential. The parents would have been upset with the teacher if he/she had said "their child" is lacking ability. The burden of motivation is erroneously placed squarely on the child. Sally Todd, in *You and the Gifted Child*, provides the following characteristics of the underachiever:

1. They have a low self-concept demonstrated by distrust, lack of concern, and even hostility toward others.
2. They often feel rejected by their family; and feel that their parents are dissatisfied with them.
3. They take little responsibility for their actions.
4. They often do not like school or their teacher, and choose companions who have the same attitude.
5. They lack motivation for academic achievement.
6. They may not have hobbies that could occupy their spare time.
7. They tend to state their goals very late, have much lower aspirations than achievers, and often choose goals that are not in line with their major interest or abilities.[6]

I spoke at a youth camp recently, and attended one of the workshops on concentration and brain control. The workshop conductor had the group form a circle, and then placed an object in the center. He then wanted all of us to see how long we could concentrate on the object without allowing distractions to enter our mind. Everyone acknowledged how difficult it was to do even for two to three minutes. He commented that the brain is a little baby and needs to be disciplined. He mimmicked how children act restless in class, crossing their legs, playing with their hands, mouth, hair, etc. I thought about free-throw shooting in basketball, where the range of accuracy is from 45 to 92 percent. What explains the differential? The ball and the distance are the same, but some shooters can control their brains and concentrate better than others.

Upon completion of that workshop, I felt that very early in school, children should be given exercises in concentration. I realized that whatever you want to achieve in life will require the ability to discipline the brain. Some people can focus talents and energy on one objective for longer periods of time than others. This ability to discipline the brain and maximize concentration may be essential in talent development. Frequently, in our home, our family plays concentration with a deck of cards turned over. Observing my sons affords me an opportunity to measure this vital ability. This talent may be essential to the release of all other talents throughout the body.

I believe the key factor in motivating Black youth for success is to "use yourself up." The search to identify and develop your talents is a lifelong process, as demonstrated by Paul Robeson, Magic Johnson, and Jeremiah Wright. Students may cheat for a grade, but when you go all of your life not knowing what your talents are — consequently not developing them — you cheat yourself. Money may not be enough to motivate all youth to work hard and get a good education. I suggest one major purpose in life is to *identify* and *develop* your *talents*.

The next chapter takes a look at the present and future employment picture. We now must begin to merge the politics of work, values, motivation, and talents into the present economy and beyond.

Chapter 5

Jobs: The Present and Beyond

Where did the jobs go? Made in Hong Kong, Korea, Taiwan, or Mexico. America has always had international interests, starting from importing slaves and natural resources from Africa to exporting over-priced or finished products back to the "Third World." The international link became more complex with OPEC oil negotiations and the rising cost of U.S. labor. Heavy industrial areas such as steel, cars, and electronics have joined with toys and clothes to be produced overseas. Simultaneously, domestic firms display "Buy American" bumper stickers. U.S. companies want their workers and consumers to be patriotic and loyal while they prostitute and imperialize the rest of the world.

This country would have very little difficulty achieving full employment if they simply created a national employment policy that would reverse the jobs lost overseas. The mistake that many well-intentioned advocates make is assuming owners have the same values as workers and consumers. Capitalists never said their objective was full employment; their first and major obsession is to make a profit, *wherever* it's possible. The contradictions of capitalism are better explained in the Marxist literature, but suffice to say, if capitalism is always looking for new frontiers and people to exploit profitably, the supply will eventually be exhausted. When owners suppress wages, they reduce available consumable dollars, consequently products are either bought with governmental subsidies to corporations and families or exported overseas.

My major reason for providing this brief overview in economic theory is to encourage workers to begin operating from their own interests. When workers enter the marketplace looking for work, we need to be clear where the values of both parties lie. Workers enter the labor force to sell their skills for the top dollar. If the owner did not value their skills or could find any other way to produce his product without it, he would. For example, I don't have any problem with athletes securing large salaries from their owners. First, if the owner can pay that kind of salary to a player, what does he pay himself. Secondly, if the owner doesn't think the player is worth it, he is not forced to sign him, *but* the player should have the opportunity to see what he is worth on the open market. Thirdly, players like Vida Blue, Reggie Jackson, Patrick Ewing, and others have documented that when they play, attendance figures increase, which is the best index to justify additional compensation. Lastly, many non-athletes are simply jealous that their chosen field does not command the same compensation; but I wonder how many critics, given the same opportunity in their occupation would pass it up, especially in sports where the average career lasts only five years.

My major suggestion to workers is to always develop your talents and skills to increase your marketability. The negotiations between owners and workers are based on different interests. Joe McDonald, twenty-year veteran at U.S. Steel in Gary has been laid off for the past six years. He is forty years old with a wife, three children, and a mortgage. Joe had moved up the ranks and had become a welder making $18.00 an hour plus benefits. Joe felt very secure on his job, expressed by his large accumulation of debt, and his not developing other skills "just in case." He never thought U.S. Steel would close or, more precisely, relocate to Korea. Joe waited for two years to be recalled while receiving unemployment benefits and union support. Over the last four years he's realized that there are few $18.00 per hour jobs in the "third wave" economy. Wages once paid in the second wave of industrialism are not being offered in the third wave of automation and the service sector. In 1960, manufacturing accounted for one out of every four jobs. By 1980 it was responsible for one out of five, and by 1990 was only one out of six. After hitting a high-water mark of about 45 percent in the 1950s, unions now claim only 22 percent of the nation's workers. Illustrated on the next page are some of the reasons why automation and the anticipated 17,000 robots per year will decrease Black employment.

Occupation	Number of Black Workers 1980	Percentage of Total Jobs Held by Blacks — 1980	Reason for Projected Decline in Employment in 1990
Cleaners and Servants	262,194	53.4%	Mechanized Commercial Cleaning Services
Clothing Ironers	46,056	40.4%	Synthetic Fibers and Automatic Pressers
Farm Laborers	151,255	16.9%	Robot Planters, Sorters and Harvesters
Packers and Wrappers	115,200	19.2%	Mechanical Sorting and Packaging
Sewers and Stitchers	156,812	19.9%	Automatic Fusing Machines
Postal Service Workers	68,970	24.2%	Electronic Mail and Optical Mail Scanners
Transit Workers	114,920	22.1%	Automatic Transportation Systems
Textile Workers	72,998	22.6%	Computer-Controlled Looms and Knitters
Typists	158,565	15.5%	Electronic Voice Transcribers
Steel Workers	63,802	14.6%	Computerized Production
Automobile Washers	33,970	21.5%	Self-Service Car Washes
Loggers	19,008	19.9%	Automatic Tree Harvesters
Bakers	13,965	10.5%	Continuous Mix Systems
Metal Molders	14,025	25.5%	Automatic Sand Slingers
Assembly Line Workers	175,864	15.2%	Industrial Robots
Paper Mill Workers	58,860	16.4%	Automatic Continuous Pulp Digestors
Boiler Tenders	9,996	14.7%	Thermostat Control Systems
Library Attendants	20,064	13.2%	Home Computer Access to Library Files
Telephone Operators	49,928	15.8%	Automatic Switching Devices
Stock Clerks	66,092	12.4%	Computerized Storage and Retrieval Systems

Welders (Joe McDonald)	78,888	11.4%	Robotic Arc Welding
Cashiers	167,832	10.8%	Universal Product Code Scanners
File Clerks	69,984	21.6%	Electronic File Retrieval
Tailors and Dressmakers	21,017	15.8%	Computer-Controlled Stitching
Messengers	15,974	16.3%	Telecommunications and Electronic Mail
Fabric Cutters	42,987	16.1%	Computer-Guided Laser Scissors
Gardeners	97,963	16.3%	Robot Lawn Mowers and Sprinklers
Key Punch Oper.	57,988	21.8%	Optical Scanners and Readers
Stenographers	9,984	15.6%	Automatic Dictation Machines
Private Mail Carriers	37,950	23.0%	Electronic Mail

Jobs Vulnerable to Robots

Farm laborers	Meat cutters
Mail carriers	Gas station attendants
Messengers	Railroad workers
Stock clerks	Ticket collectors
Food counter workers	Mass transit workers
Steel workers	Utility meter readers
Dishwashers	Bottlers and canners
Key punch operators	Fork lift operators
Bank tellers	Payroll clerks
Checkout clerks	File clerks
Telephone operators	Textile workers
Assembly line workers	Shipping clerks
Parking lot attendants	Elevator operators
Garbage collectors	Freight handlers
Automobile workers	Clothing ironers
Welders	Stenographers
Gardeners[2]	

Joe McDonald's major question is, where are the jobs for the future? This is a question not only asked by workers, but by employment counselors and forecasters. The advancement in technology supposedly will create new jobs to replace extinct positions. High-tech should provide more leisure time, and accelerate the growth in recreation, services, and specialty shops. Listed below is a table showing those areas with the fastest growth rate followed by a table showing those occupations with the greatest aggregate increase projected for 1990.

Projected Employment

Occupation	Growth 1978-1990
Computer programmers	73.6%
Systems analysts	107.8
Electronic technicians	45.4
Vocational trainers	26.5
Laboratory technicians	43.9
Crane operators	40.4
Appliance repairers	24.1
Health care technicians	45.0
Auto body repairers	27.0
Physical therapists	57.5
X-Ray technicians	47.4
Bulldozer operators	57.0
Travel agents	55.6
Paralegals	132.4
Plumbers	20.0
Nurses	50.3
Accountants	32.7
Law clerks	44.0
Firemen	22.7
Lithographers	45.8
Electricians	24.6
Tax preparers	64.5
Mechanics	29.7
Policemen	23.23

Forty Occupations with
Largest Projected Growth: 1982-1995

Occupation	Change in total employment (in thousands)	Percent of total job growth	Percent change
Building custodians	779	3.0	27.5
Cashiers	744	2.9	47.4
Secretaries	719	2.8	29.5
General clerks, office	696	2.7	29.6
Salesclerks	685	2.7	23.5
Nurses, registered	642	2.5	48.9
Waiters and waitresses	562	2.2	33.8
Teachers, kindergarten and elementary	511	2.0	37.4
Truck drivers	425	1.7	26.5
Nursing aides and orderlies	423	1.7	4.8
Sales representatives, technical	386	1.5	29.3
Accountants and auditors	344	1.3	40.2
Automotive mechanics	324	1.3	38.3
Supervisors of blue collar workers	319	1.2	26.6
Kitchen helpers	305	1.2	35.9
Guards and doorkeepers	300	1.2	47.3
Food preparation and service workers, fast food restaurants	297	1.2	36.7
Managers store	292	1.1	30.1
Carpenters	247	1.0	28.6
Electrical and electronic technicians	222	.9	60.7
Licensed practical nurses	220	.9	37.1
Computer systems analysts	217	.8	85.3
Electrical engineers	209	.8	65.3
Computer programmers	205	.8	76.9
Maintenance repairers, general utility	193	.8	27.8
Helpers trades	190	.7	31.2
Receptionist	189	.7	48.8
Electricians	173	.7	31.8
Physicians	163	.7	34.0
Clerical supervisors	162	.6	34.6
Computer operators	160	.6	75.8
Sales representatives nontechnical	160	.6	27.4
Lawyers	159	.6	34.3

Stock clerks, stockroom and warehouse	156	.6	18.8
Typists	155	.6	15.7
Delivery and route workers	153	.6	19.2
Bookkeepers, hand	152	.6	15.9
Cooks, restaurants	149	.6	42.3
Bank tellers	142	.6	30.0
Cooks, short order, specialty and fast food	141	.6	32.2[4]

It is not my desire to disappoint or confuse Black youth in a book designed to motivate, but as I have said in previous chapters, I do not believe you can motivate Black youth with a lie. Those areas with the fastest rate are primarily high-tech which require a math and science background. I encourage Black youth to be prepared in these subjects. The complexity lies in the fact that high-tech will probably represent only seven percent of the labor force; of the top ten occupations in *total* numbers, only nursing and teaching require a college degree, and the leading occupations are custodians, cashiers, and secretaries.

How do we motivate Joe McDonald and Black youth with the above analysis? There will be increased competition for the "elite" jobs of the future. A college degree will remain a valued commodity, but its stock will increase if its concentration is in engineering, computers, accounting, education, medicine, or marketing. Specialists in word processing, paralegals, auto and appliance repairers, plumbers, electricians and carpenters will be lucrative occupations. There will be a widening gap between the haves and have-nots, with a small number needed in the growth fields and a larger number needed in low-skilled areas. The major advice any counselor should give to youth would be for them to familiarize themselves with the above charts, remain flexible, continue to learn new skills, and understand that the marketplace between owner and worker is based on negotiated interests and values.

One of the frequent comments heard from "the political right" and some Blacks who blame the victims is the numerous pages of want ads. The sentiment expressed is that the problem is not unemployment, but workers lacking "third wave" skills. I encourage everyone to play "the want ad exercise." The *Sunday Chicago Tribune* may have 20 pages of employment advertisements; if you called every position you may find half of them have been filled through their internal apparatus. (Often times personnel departments publicly show a position to protect themselves from charges of discriminatory practices, while all along they knew the position was to be filled from within.) Secondly, for many inner-city residents the jobs are either not accessible by public transportation or are so far by car or bus that an inordinate amount of salary is spent on transportation. I see numerous fast-food chains advertising in the suburbs for part-time help. But can we blame Black youth for not being able to reach it? Or adults for not feeling minimum-wage salaries warrant four hours each day of commuting? There is no excuse though for idleness, and the need to learn new skills and volunteer time in the Black community.

After eliminating jobs that no longer exist and/or are inaccessible, we come to those engineering, computer, accounting, medical, marketing, word processing, and paralegal positions that some of us are qualified for, but which require one to five years experience. Where and when are Joe McDonald and Black youth going to be able to learn the skill and gain experience simultaneously? Black youth, both qualified and unqualified, then call the few remaining positions not affected by the above.

On a more optimistic note are the many job training and manpower programs nationwide providing an excellent service to our community. I have had the fortunate opportunity to observe and interview numerous directors about their full range of services. While there is no question that a greater commitment of time and money are needed from the government, these directors also said that their programs are often *under-utilized* by their constituency. Many of these programs provide GED certificates, training in high-tech areas, self-esteem, grooming and interviewing techniques, and job placement.

The Neighborhood Institute, based in Chicago, provides an eight-week course that concentrates on appearance, communication, and thinking skills. Employers have targeted these areas along with technical skills as their major concerns. The Institute helps clients in goal clarification, resume preparation, and interviewing strategies. Here are some of their "Stress Interview Questions" and the major reasons why people lose their jobs.

STRESS INTERVIEW QUESTIONS

What are your short-range objectives?

What are your long-range objectives?

What can you do for us that someone else cannot do?

Why should we hire you?

Can you work under pressure, deadlines, etc.?

What is your philosophy of management?

Do you prefer staff or line work? Why?

What kind of salary are you worth?

What are your five biggest accomplishments in: Your present or last job? Your career so far?

Why didn't you do better in college? What is your biggest strength/weakness?

How long would it take you to make a contribution to our firm?

How long would you stay with us?

How do you feel about people from minority groups?

If you could start again, what would you do differently?

What new goals or objectives have you established recently?

How have you changed the nature of your job?

What position do you expect to have in five years?

What do you think of your boss?

Why haven't you obtained a job so far?

What features of your previous jobs have you disliked?

Would you describe a few situations in which your work was criticized?

Would you object to working for a woman?

Some of your experience isn't related to the position. How can you compensate for that?

How would you evaluate your present job?

Do you generally speak to people before they speak to you?

How would you describe the essence of success?

What was the last book you read? Movie you saw? Sporting event you attended?

In your present position, what problems have you identified that had previously been overlooked?

What interests you most about the position we have? The least?

Don't you feel you might be better off in a different size company? Different type company?

Why aren't you earning more at your job?

Will you be out to take your boss's job?
Are you creative? Give an example.
Are you analytical? Give an example.
Are you a leader? Give an example.
How would you describe your own performance?
Have you helped increase sales? How?
Have you helped reduce costs? How?
What do your subordinates think of you?
Have you fired people before?
Have you hired people before? What do you look for?
Why do you want to work for us?
If you had your choice of jobs and companies, where would you go?
What other types of jobs are you considering? What companies?
Why do you feel you have top management potential?
Tell us about yourself. Are you conceptual? Give an example.
If you had only one question that you could ask of me, what would it be?

Why People Lose Their Jobs:

1. Coming to work late or leaving early
2. Taking too many breaks or staying too long on them
3. Being dishonest or stealing from the boss
4. Missing too many days from work
5. Not following company rules
6. Not getting along well with others
7. Being lazy and not doing a fair work share
8. Not willing to train for the job
9. Doing messy or incomplete work
10. Being too slow or not trying to improve[5]

In looking at the chapter on jobs, we should not only be concerned about the kinds of positions, but where they are located. We all have heard about industry's move south and west toward the Sun Belt. Listed are the high and low growth rate states.

High-Growth States Through 1993

	Annual Percentage Growth	Total Growth
Arizona	2.94	351,560
Nevada	2.8	7,135,680
Florida	2.67	1,167,130
New Mexico	2.55	137,790
Colorado	2.49	371,700
Georgia	2.4	5,614,610
Texas	2.4	11,658,140
California	2.39	2,626,310
New Hampshire	2.30	100,060
Virginia	2.29	547,490

Low-Growth States

	Percentage Growth	Total Growth
Delaware	1.65	46,370
New Jersey	1.63	544,650
Ohio	1.61	711,790
Maine	1.59	70,320
Illinois	1.57	762,000
West Virginia	1.55	97,900
Dist. of Columbia	1.40	88,870
Pennsylvania	1.31	618,300
New York	1.25	957,050
North Dakota	1.22	32,590[6]

The high-growth states have a much smaller percentage of Blacks than the industrial Northeast and Midwest. Statistical tables can also be confusing. For example, let's compare Arizona with New York. The rate of growth for Arizona is twice the rate of New York, but New York will produce almost three times as many jobs over the decade; but the greater population in New York will increase competition. Joe McDonald lives in Gary, and, like so many other cities that were dependent on one industry, it has become a virtual ghost town. (Richard Hatcher needs to be commended for the additional resources brought into Gary.) It is often said Black people are landlocked, living primarily in the largest thirty cities regardless of their economic conditions.

The decision to relocate is complex. Blacks obviously proved they were not landlocked in the 1920s with the large migrations northward. Recently there have been traces of a return migration southward and to California. The Black population in the South still represents 53 percent of its total. One of the major strengths of the Black community is the extended family. Blacks are less inclined than other groups to move cross-country and leave behind relatives for a few more dollars. I am reminded of the White affluent suburb of Dallas, and the rising rate of teenage suicides. A high school counselor said that she had not seen a grandparent out of 3,000 students, and one of the teenage suicide victims, who hung himself to a tree, left a note saying, "This was the only thing that had *roots*." Relocation is a middle-class phenomenon that assumes you have skills and/or a position on the other end. A person is less likely to relocate to Arizona with no skills.

Lastly, I'd like to look at the military, specifically, the U.S. Army and its impact on our youth. Their favorite slogan is "Be all that you can be," and for a youth struggling to graduate from high school with an economy as complex as previously described, it *seems* like the best thing to do. I have seen students drop out of school and return for a GED with the sole purpose to become enlistment. I have even seen cases where our youth have been registered without GED or diploma! There are mothers who, after eighteen years of "loving" (unconditional love creating irresponsibility) their sons versus "raising" (unconditional love creating responsiblity and self-actualization) them, *give* them to the Army in hopes they will make him a responsible man. The enlistment meetings remind me of the EMR (Educable Mentally Retarded) meetings that took place when Black boys were nine years old. Unfortunately, at this meeting, nine years later, many parents don't even attend. Parents who have participated in these military meetings, have told me their presence may very well have determined whether their son was placed on the front line or in electronics. If the parent and the larger Black community had been more involved, challenged the school, curriculum, and the teacher about the disproportionate number of Black boys placed in EMR, this subsequent army meeting might have been unnecessary. For every isolated "success" story in the Army, I can provide nine that were failures. Blacks are 12 percent of the population, but are 33 percent of the Army, were 41 percent of the deaths in Vietnam, and only 7 percent of the officers.[7]

In conclusion, I did not want you to understand the politics of work, change your values, become motivated to learn, identify and develop your talents, for you to *look* for a job. If you must do that, I hope this chapter has been of some assistance. Many counselors confine their advice to seeking employment. I view this as a temporary phase with the ultimate destination being developing a career, starting your own business, and making the Black community strong and viable. I believe the best way to motivate and prepare Black youth to work is to identify and develop their talents.

A Good education should make you economically independent and self-sufficient by teaching you skills to make a product or provide a service.

Chapter 6

How to Become
Economically Self-Sufficient

I travel on airplanes about two or three days a week, and have noticed that the "world runners" — White men — make up 90 percent of the occupancy, with the remaining 10 percent divided among White and Black women and Black men. It hurts me sometimes to see all these financially successful White men and so few Black men when I can so vividly remember the night before college graduation, White men were still having panty raids and beer fights, but because of their white privileges, have risen high up in the corporate ranks. I will never forget one particular trip where two White men were talking about their professions. (I wish more Blacks, especially those in college, would talk about career options and possible business ventures.) One of the men was a personnel recruiter for a firm that produces nails. When most of us see nails, that is probably all we see.

Let me share from the above experience what I see. I envision one to three men who decided years ago that they wanted to work for themselves, and they sat down and created Nails, Inc. Years later, this company not only sends its staff on expensive recruiting trips, but has an engineering department charged with combining raw materials to achieve product quality and safety specifications. It also has a purchasing department responsible for securing all needed materials, and which is very much aware that one part missing could cause costly delays. Nails, Inc. has an accounting department assigned to oversee the budget and operate the disbursements, receivables, income and balance sheet statements, and plan investment strategies. The company also has a marketing division which handles its print advertisement, administers the sales force, and provides the company with a good image. I see a million square foot plant which also has a maintenance staff. When I see a nail, I recognize a company behind it that employs over 500 people with a $5 million dollar payroll, which multiplies itself four times by contributing additional jobs to the city of Nailville. It is called Nailville because it is the largest employer in town, pays thousands of dollars in taxes, has three officers on various municipal boards, and its former CEO (Chief Executive Officer) and founder is the present mayor. What do you see when you see a nail? I see the above that started with one to three men who had a vision.

What keeps so many Blacks away from starting their own businesses? George Subira, in *Black Folks' Guide to Making Big Money in America*, says a "good job." He further states:

> to be Black and have a "good job" usually means you went to college, competed against other blacks and whites for the job and won, you have responsibility, proud of your social image, and lastly and most dangerously have been promised advancement and security. Now for this company man to risk all of this to operate his own business for many is inconceivable. A Black with a "good job" for more than ten years is very much like a convict who has been in prison for ten years. Neither one of them can make it on "the outside" regardless of how much strength and character they demonstrate "inside."[1]

I believe we need a new generation of youth, motivated, talented, with a budget based on needs, who will have the confidence to start their own businesses. Employers have more faith in us than we have in ourselves. Why would they hire us, if they did not believe our contribution to the company would pay not only our salary but operating expenses, and help bring substantial profits. Many of us talk a good "black game", but would rather someone else have the responsibility of Friday payroll. It is amazing that Carter G. Woodson's writings from fifty years ago are still so applicable.

> In the schools of business administration Negroes are trained exclusive in the psychology and economics of Wall Street and are, therefore, made to despise the opportunities to run ice wagons, push banana carts, and sell peanuts among their own people. Foreigners, who have not studied economics, but have studied Negroes, take up this business and grow rich.[2]

The accuracy of this historical quote is astonishing. Our talented tenth prefer to work downtown, and the few Black businesses we have are often operated by those lacking in economic principles. How nice it would be if our talented tenth had the vision to "do for self" instead of leaving the business opportunities to the Jews, Arabs, Asians and Koreans who now operate in the Black community.

Many of us believe that business is comprised solely of capital, labor, and a physical plant. While these are essential resources, what precedes all of this is attitude or "social capital." Glen Loury coined the phrase, to refer to:

> those institutions within a community, that generate economic dividends, by shaping the values and attitudes of individuals. There is ample evidence that the home and church can yield significant economic benefits. We discovered that young men who had been taught to aspire to relatively high-status occupations, later in life worked nearly 25 percent more weeks per year than otherwise similar youths who had no such aspirations. It was revealed that those who reported religion is important in their lives worked about 15 percent more weeks per year than comparable youths who lacked a religious background.[3]

There are numerous books promoting positive mental attitude (PMA). Some of the most important attitudes to possess are: good self-esteem, think big, take risks, avoid use of the word "can't," accept responsibility for your actions, work hard, become knowledgeable, monitor your time, keep healthy and energetic, be decisive, and interact with positive peers.

What should a motivated youth do when he/she is out of work? First, I believe all of us should learn how to make a product and provide a service. When you can't do either, you have to ask someone for a job. If you can make a product or provide a service, you will reduce the chance of being unemployed. A good education should make you independent and self-sufficient by teaching these skills. I would recommend that our youth learn both a blue-collar and white-collar skill. We need to quit choosing between the philosophy of DuBois and Booker T. Washington and accept both. Many white-collar professionals look down at blue-collar workers until they have to pay $30.00 plus per hour to plumbers, carpenters, and electricians. The latter have so much contempt for the scholars, they seldom master the business side of their professions, which would enable them to secure large governmental contracts requiring an extensive amount of paperwork. Secondly, I would encourage our youth to understand the field of selling. I have found many people are afraid of sales and public speaking. I believe one reason is they did not believe in what they were selling or speaking. I am against students first encountering public speaking with a topic they do not believe, and I am not in favor of youths and adults selling any product indiscriminately. You must first ask yourself, what do I like? Secondly, can I make any money selling it? And lastly, how many other people can I convince to buy what I like?

For example, most people think I am a writer, public speaker, and salesman, but I don't write, speak, or sell everything. My next book will be titled *Marketing Black Consciousness*; my doctoral dissertation was "The Marketability of Black Literature." I write and speak about the liberation of Black people, and sell books and related items committed to that position. I am not as effective writing, talking, or selling a product or concept I do not believe in.

I encourage Black youth to understand sales. This field is the basic way goods and services are distributed, consequently it employs large numbers and offers unlimited income. But please remember, only sell what you enjoy, then it won't feel like work, but an extension of yourself. We have too many people working and selling things they do not enjoy. As mentioned earlier, a major hinderance to starting your own business is a "good job"; a major obstacle to sales is the desire for a guaranteed salary. Many people who lack confidence in their abilities would prefer a guaranteed salary, versus working on commissions with unlimited income. George Subira recommends that those conservative-minded individuals try sales part-time, so that their bills are placed on the "good job," while they try sales. I also encourage you to take advantage of the creative and innovative marketing plans companies have designed, where you not only sell products, but have other people selling them for you.

The first step in starting your own business is to have a positive attitude, followed by identifying something you enjoy selling. Then we must understand the value of money, real estate, and taxes. Black youths often go to school from pre-kindergarten through twelfth grade, plus undergraduate and above, and are not knowledgeable of the fundamentals of this economy. Most Blacks work harder for their money than their money works for them. Many of us value cars more than real estate, and we pay more taxes while earning less income. I find no better way to motivate Black youth than to encourage them to use their talents for themselves by

Selling is the way goods and services are distributed; it employs large numbers and offers unlimited income.

understanding money, real estate, and taxes.

The greatest hindrance to investment is again the desire for a guarantee. Blacks, more than most people, would prefer a "guaranteed" 5 percent interest from a bank or savings and loan, or 8 to 10 percent interest from a certificate of deposit with strict time limitations, than investing in money market, mutual funds, common stocks, leasing, or real estate. I wonder if we ever ask the banks and savings and loans institutions which pay us 5 to 10 percent interest, where do they make their 15 to 50 percent interest? Just as employers do with our labor, banks have more confidence with our money in "unguaranteed" places than we do. The formula for investment is time-rate-capital, the combination of investing young with a good rate of return with as little capital as fifty dollars per month can provide a college education or the capital needed to start Nails, Inc.

In a book titled *Motivating and Preparing Black Youth For Success,* I do not want to provide an in-depth analysis of business theory, but I do encourage you to read *The Power of Money Dynamics* by Venita Van Caspel, *Black Folks' Guide to Making Big Money in America* by George Subira, *101 Businesses You Can Start and Run with Less than $1,000* by H.S. Kahm, and *How to Become a Successful Consultant in Your Own Field* by Hubert Bermont.

Finally, on the idea of starting your own business, you must ask yourself, "Am I starting the business to serve the customer or to provide myself a means of employment where I am the boss and do whatever, whenever, and wherever I feel?" Many Blacks think that having your own business makes you the boss with no accountability; while in contrast, many Whites understand that the customer is the most important asset of the business, and that a harmonious, cohesive staff is necessary to provide customer satisfaction.

I remember two "negotiations" I was in with Black businesses. The first was a pizza shop advertising free pop with a family-size pizza. I ordered the largest size available in deep dish, which exceeded the dollar value of a family-size thin crust. I calmly explained that the ad did not specify thin crust, that I had ordered the largest deep dish and it had a greater dollar value, and, in addition, I was a frequent customer. The second example was a owner of a facility our school wanted to rent for classroom purposes. We knew the owner was having financial problems; the space was not being used, and we offered a fair price for rental. In both cases the owners took a attitude of a HNIC (Head Negro in Charge) with them holding the trump card. They didn't realize how valuable I was to their operation, and treated me as an enemy rather than the person who puts bread on their table. It takes a lot of my political commitment to continue to support these kinds of businesses. These same owners will be the first to condemn the Black community for lack of support, without ever looking at themselves.

Listed below are a few good reasons to start your own business:

1) An opportunity to work longer hours and to give more of your love, creativity and talent to a task than what is provided by most job situations;

2) An opportunity to receive a fair return (money and other benefits) for such additional work output in ways that are not tied to "wage guidelines" or other artificial, limiting, subjective or arbitrary decisions by others;

3) An opportunity to build something of lasting value that can be sold or passed on to heirs; (A job's benefits obviously last only as long as the job lasts, and cannot be passed on to anyone.)

4) An opportunity to gain additional tax advantages and build a substantial net worth;

5) An opportunity to employ others;

6) An opportunity to give some kind of community service;

7) An opportunity to attract other business opportunities or financial investors;

8) An opportunity for a degree of independence, "freedom," and a greater sense of security than jobs can usually provide;

9) An opportunity for a significant identity so that your fellow man can know you exist, and appreciate you and work with you.

My desire has been to motivate and prepare Black youth for success. We are not a lazy people, but a proud people who would like to be compensated fairly. We have excelled in every industry where we've been allowed to participate; we have the capacity to be good ballplayers or scholars if given the opportunity. A large part of the problem has been an erosion of our values. The larger society, and Black youth specifically, often want to "feel good and look good" at any cost. Values such as hard work, savings and the liberation of Black people can only be taught by concerned adults who are willing to compete against the onslaught of media bombardment.

Many Black youths have lost the desire to learn because they have not been encouraged to ask questions and to develop critical thinking skills. Many youths have determined that the motive for schools is to get good grades by whatever means; securing employment is based more on who you know than what you know. We are not going to motivate and prepare Black youth without being honest about the complexity of school, diet, media, and economy. The problem may not be with Black youths, but with adults who don't know how to develop teenagers.

Unfortunately, many Black youths spend their entire lives neither finding nor developing their God-given talents. I believe the best way to motivate and prepare Black youth is to encourage them to "use themselves up." Many adults have already discovered the void in their lives thinking cars, clothes, appliances, drugs, and sex could make up for working a job. I have attempted pragmatically to show how Black youth with limited resources can discover and develop their talents. This same pragmatism was used in exploring employment opportunities. This last chapter was an attempt to show our youth who are motivated, talented, and operating on a "needs" value system, how they can start their own business and contribute to the vitality of the Black community.

EPILOGUE

I often think about what I would like to do for the future. Two project ideas have been generated by this book. Just as with *Countering the Conspiracy to Destroy Black Boys*, which helped promote the continuance of Simba program (activities designed by men to take boys through the rites of passage) and are now operating in over fifteen cities across the country, I'd like to share these two projects, either for your assistance to me, and/or your development in your respective city.

Kuumba (Creativity) House

This is a talent center located in the Black community. It provides one general location to learn and develop hobbies and talents. The few places in our community that provide talent development concentrate primarily on basketball, football, baseball, track, singing, dancing, and sometimes piano. Kuumba House may consider these but, with limited dollars and space will concentrate on science, mathematics, debate, writing, spelling, art, mechanics, gymnastics, marital arts, drama, and musical instruments.

There is a fear in many Black youths of competing academically. This is reflected in a lack of competitive academic activities and an over-abundance of athletic events. The Kuumba House will not only offer all these "talent centers" but will provide "healthy competition" to stimulate its growth.

The School of Kujichagulia (Self-Determination)

This school is designed for the aggressive learner who wants a hands-on approach to learning. Many Black students who ask questions or demand relevancy, are labeled EMR (Educable Mentally Retarded) or BD (Behavioral Disorder) and end up in prisons. I believe some of our best minds are incarcerated. The requirements to enter would be a high diploma or its equivalent. While we would like to attract the talented tenth, most of them have the ability to make it in college. Our focus would be attracting those youth that normally might not succeed in "traditional" institutions.

The objective of the school would be to teach how to produce a good or provide a service that can be developed into a business. Upon completion of all course work, the students, with the assistance of faculty members, will design a business plan that will be presented to banks. The school will not only provide the curriculum to achieve this goal, but will align itself with the financial community to secure financing. The school will co-sign all loans. Board members and alumni from the school will provide an excellent pool of networking which will enhance contract procurement and continued business expertise.

FOOTNOTES

Chapter 1

1) Marable, Manning. *How Capitalism Underdeveloped Black America.* Boston: South End Press, 1983, pp 3,7.
2) U. S. Dept. of Commerce Bureau of Census, America's Black Population 1984, p4.
3) U.S. Dept. of Labor, Bureau of Labor Statistics, Special Labor Force Report 225.
4) Thomas, Veronica. "Black Youth Unemployment." Issues, Concerns and Strategies For Change. *Urban Research Review*, Vol. 9, No. 3, 1984 pp 1-4.
   Curwood, Steve. "Minorities Face Grim Employment Future," Chicago Sun Times, November 9, 1983, p74.
5) Chicago Tribune, "For Some Jobless, Survival Means They Steal and Deal," July 16, Section 2, pp3.
6) Wilhelm, Sidney. *Who Needs the Negro.* New York: Doubleday 1971, pp XIII, 222,223.
7) Colt, Allan. "Orthornolecular Approach to the Treatment of Children with Behavior Disorder and Learning Disabilities." *Journal of Applied Nutrition*, 1973, Vol. 25, Nos. 1 & 2, Winter, pp. 25-36.
8) Postman, Neil. *The Disappearance of Childhood.* New York: Delacorte Press, 1982, pp 10,13,14,18.
9) Goodlad, John. *A Place Called School.* New York: McGraw Hill, 1984, p.12.
10) Thomas. O.P. Cit, p3.
11) Terkel, Studs. *Working.* New York: Pantheon Books 1972, pp 449,521.
12) McDaniels, Carl. "The Work/Leisure Connection." Vocational Guidance Quarterly, Vol 33, No. I, pp 35-42.
13) Toffler, Alvin. *The Third Wave.* New York: William Morrow, 1980, pp. 367-376.

Chapter 2

1) Yates, Ronald. "East meets West — and Finds Decadence." *Chicago Tribune*, August 4, 1984, Section I, p. 5.
2) Simmons, Richard. *The Crucial Element.* Chicago: Richard Simmons, 1985, pix.
3) Amini, Johari. "Behavior and Its Value Base." *Black Books Bulletin*, Volume 4, No. 3, 1976, p.43.
4) Wobogo, Vulinedela. "Two Cradle Theory and the Origin of White Racism." *Black Books Bulletin*, Volume 4, No. 4, 1976, p.23.

FOOTNOTES

5) Amini Op. Cit pp. 40-41.

6) Lasch, Christopher. *The Culture of Narcissism.* New York: W.W. Norton, 1979, pp 30-31, 101, 106-107, 137.

7) Black Child Care Conference, Columbus, Ohio, September 1981.

8) Karenga, Maulana. *Kwanzaa, Origin, Concepts, Practice.* Los Angeles: Kawaida Publication, p.1.

9) Jordan Val. *The Black Value System.* (Chicago: Trinity Church, 1981).

Chapter 3

1) Kunjufu, Jawanza. *Countering The Conspiracy to Destroy Black Boys.* Chicago: African American Images, 1983, p. 7.

2) Morgan, Harry. "How Schools Fail Black Children." *Social Policy,* Jan-Feb, 1980, pp. 49-54.

3) U. S. Department of Labor, Bureau of Labor Statistics Press Release pp. 79-90.

4) *Chicago Tribune.* "A Reading on School's Freshman Class." April 28, 1985, Tempo Section.

5) Minority College Report Manual. "The High Cost of Dropping Out," Education Section.

6) Packard, Vance. *Our Endangered Children.* Boston: Little, Brown and Co., 1983 p. 16.

Chapter 4

1) *Holy Bible,* King James Version, Matthew 25:15. 29

2) Bloom, Benjamin. *Developing Talent In Young People.* New York: Ballantine, 1985, pp. 3-5.

3) Howard, Jeff and Hammond, Ray. "The Intellectual Inferiority Game." Boston: The Efficacy Committee, 1985, pp. 2, 4, and 8.

4) Holland, John. *The Self Directed Search.* Palo Alto: Consulting Psychologists Press, 1977, p. 2-3.

5) Black Enterprise. "Everything You'd Like to Give Your Kids But Weren't Sure You Could Afford." October, 1985, pp. 48-50.

6) Todd, Sally. *You and the Gifted Child.* Springfield: Charles Thomas Publishers, 1983 p. 111.

Chapter 5

1) Quinlan, Tim. "The new high-tech employment market will offer many jobs at mini-wages." *Chicago Sun-Times,* May 23, 1983, p. 29

2) Cross, Theodore. *The Black Power Imperative.* New York: Faulkner, 1984, pp. 448-449, 622.

FOOTNOTES

3) ibid. p. 623.

4) *Monthly Labor Review*, "Occupational Employment Projections to 1995," p. 45.

5) The Neighborhood Institute Career Education and Employment Cennter, "Try-out Employment Placement Program." Participant's Manual, Chicago.

6) Saunders, Dick. "Sun Belt big winner in jobs survey." *Chicago Sun-Times*, August 26, 1984, p. 55.

7) Staples, Robert. *Black Masculinity*. San Francisco: Black Scholar Press, 1982, p. 24.

8) U.S. Department of Commerce Bureau of Census "America's Black Population," 1983, pp 23-24.

Chapter 6

1) Subira, George. *Black Folks' Guide to Making Big Money in America*. Newark: Very Serious Business Enterprises, p. 62.

2) Woodson, Carter G. *Miseducation of the Negro*. Washington: Associated Publishers, 1933, p. 5.

3) Loury, Glenn. "New Dividends Through Social Capital." *Black Enterprise*, July 1985, p. 36.

4) Subira, p. 156.

INDEX

Adolescence 10, 19, 30, 32
Advertising 10, 16, 19-20
Africa 17, 38
Alcohol 8, 19
Amini, Johari 16-18, 20-21
Arabs 61
Asians 45, 61

Bible 35
Black Enterprise 41
Black men 15-17, 19
Black women 15, 18, 20
Bloom, Benjamin 37
"Buppies" 5

Capitalism 2, 8, 45
Chicago Public Schools 26-27
Childhood 10
Church 22, 38, 41
Cigarettes 19
Communication 9
Competition 23, 38
Consumer 16, 19
Countering the Conspiracy
    to Destroy Black Boys i, 11, 25
Credit Cards 19
Cult 13

Depression (1930) 12
Developing Positive Self Images
    and Discipline in Black
    Children i
Diet 9
Diop, Cheikh 17-18
dropout rate 26-27
drugs 6-7, 27-28
DuBois, W.E.B. 61

Educable Mentally Retarded
    (EMR) 56, 67
Efficacy Committee 38
European-American 10, 17

Flextime 12
"Fortune 500" 30

Fourth Grade Failure Syndrome 25

Gangs 7
GED 1, 52, 56
Grades 28-29
Grand Lodge of Wa'set 2, 29
    Growth rate states 55

Hatcher, Richard 55
High-tech 49-51
Hispanic-American 10
History 32-33
Hobbies 42

Inner attainment 41
Investment 22, 63

Jackson, Michael 36, 43
Jordan, Val 23-24

Kahm, H.S. 64
Karenga, Maulana 23-24
Kuumba House 67

Lasch, Christopher 18-19
Loury, Glen 61

Marable, Manning 2
Melting-pot theory 8
Military 56
Minorities 4
Morgan, Harry 26

NAACP 38
Native-American 2
Neighborhood Institute 52
Nguzo Saba 24
Northern Cradle 17

Peer group 1, 22, 31
Positive Mental Attitude (PMA) 61-62
Postman, Neil 10
Prince (Purple Rain) 43
Pyramids 2, 33